T. E. Hill

Money Found

Recovered from its hiding-places

T. E. Hill

Money Found
Recovered from its hiding-places

ISBN/EAN: 9783744726993

Printed in Europe, USA, Canada, Australia, Japan

Cover: Foto ©Suzi / pixelio.de

More available books at **www.hansebooks.com**

MONEY FOUND:

Recovered From Its Hiding-Places, and Put Into Circulation
Through Confidence In Government Banks.

BY

THOMAS E. HILL,

*Author of "Hill's Manual of Social and Business Forms," "Hill's Album of
Biography," "Hill's Guide," "The Hill Banking System," etc., etc.*

———

REVISED EDITION WITH

A Glossary of Financial Terms,

AND

GENERAL INFORMATION RELATING TO FINANCE.

———

CHICAGO:
CHARLES H. KERR & COMPANY
1894.

PREFACE.

No apology is necessary for the writing of this book. There come periods when money goes into hiding and business of all kinds is depressed. It is then that the workman is discharged and the people who are compelled to go into enforced idleness are obliged to sell, in order to maintain existence, their properties at a great reduction in value, while the people who have money at command at these times, buy at their own price and thus rapidly increase their fortunes.

Like the arrival of a pestilence among the ignorant and savage nations, the people have come to regard these periods of business depression as inevitable, and during the seasons of financial panic stand in mute wonderment at the general prostration of business, feeling themselves powerless to avert the calamity.

The writer of this is clear in his convictions that these conditions need not exist; that the cause is easily understood, and the remedy for this disturbance may be as easily applied. Under these circumstances duty demands the writing and the publishing of this book.

Full in the belief that the general public will accept the theory here advanced and that its practical application will be beneficial to the people, this work is given to the public.

INDEX TO CONTENTS.

8   INDEX TO CONTENTS

CHAPTER I.

WORK ON EVERY SIDE TO BE DONE, HOUSES TO BE BUILT,
FIELDS TO BE TILLED, ROADS TO BE IMPROVED, GREAT IM-
PROVEMENTS TO BE CARRIED FORWARD—WORKMEN ON ALL
SIDES TO DO THIS WORK, WHO NOW STAND IN IDLENESS.
—WHY NOT GIVE THEM IMMEDIATE EMPLOYMENT?

Reader, you have doubtless seen, during the years
when financial panics have prevailed, great numbers
of people standing in idleness because of being discharged from manufactories and other places where
their labors were apparently not required. At the same
time there could be seen, all over the country, in the
poorer districts of the great cities and in the inferior
homes of the rural population, the evident demand
for the work of these idlers, in order that people
might have the reasonable comforts of life.

In the public parks of the cities lounged a ragged
multitude, on the main traveled roads of the country
districts tramped a hungry horde of men—all idle.
The roads over which the tramps traveled were almost
impassable, the house where the beggar got a scanty
dinner was lacking in nearly all the conveniences
which make home desirable.

What waste of human effort! With half the labor
the tramps expend, in going from one portion of the
country to another, in the vain search for work, those
roads, over which they walked, would have turned to

boulevards. A quarter of the time, which the mechanics waste in idleness, expended in production, and every person would be well fed, clothing would be abundant, and the homes of the people would be comfortable and luxurious.

What evident lack of proper management! On every hand is the work to be done, rivers to be made navigable, fields to be fertilized, roads to be improved, houses to be built. The raw materials are waiting for the workmen, the trees stand uncut in the forest, the ore is waiting for the miner, the clay is ready to be moulded into brick and the millions of acres of fertile lands are untilled; and all this while the hundreds of thousands of idle workmen, properly directed and given full opportunity for active employment, would change these conditions, bringing plenty and comfort where there is at present enforced idleness and destitution.

Is it possible to radically reform this order of things? Let us see. Here is a great store filled to repletion with products of every description that tend to make life comfortable. Within a mile of this is a neighborhood where all of these goods are immediately required by several thousand people. The merchant complains because he cannot sell these goods; the people complain because they cannot buy them.

There is a missing link here: What is it?

The means and the medium of exchange are absent.

What is the medium of exchange and where is it?

CHAPTER II.

WHAT IS MONEY?—WHAT WILL BE THE MONEY OF THE FUTURE?—MONEY THE BLOOD OF COMMERCE, THE BANK THE HEART.—THE HEART MUST BE STRONG AND BLOOD CIRCULATE FREELY OR SICKNESS AND DEATH RESULT. —QUANTITY NOT SO IMPORTANT AS REGULARITY OF CIRCULATION IN ORDER TO SECURE HEALTH.

Any article which may be selected by a people as a means of exchange, may be termed money. The ancients used their lower animals for this purpose, an ox being worth a certain number of sheep, etc. Afterwards leather, as a representative of animals, came into use; and subsequently gold, silver and copper coins were adopted by the civilized world. As civilization has gone forward, in the most advanced nations, paper has largely come to represent coin. The inference is, as we compare the past with the present, that the great bulk of the medium of exchange, denominated money, will not be a commodity like metal, which is subject to fluctuations in value, but will be paper.

Whatever is adopted, that article should have the widest opportunity for circulation.

Money is to the Nation what blood is to the physical system. It may be termed the blood of commerce while the heart is the bank. Money performs a service, in the commercial affairs of the country, very similar to blood in the body. It must have the privilege of coming with regularity from the extremes of the country to the heart, which is the bank, to be there, in abundance, ready, as it is required, to go back again to the extremes.

In its action it is remarkably like the workings of the heart. As blood goes out through the arteries it is fresh, strong and gives vigor to the body. Having done its appointed work it comes quietly back in the veins to be vivified by the fresh air of the lungs, and thence to start afresh again, out from the heart giving health and strength through the arteries.

In like manner fresh, bright money goes out from the bank through the arteries of commerce, giving life and vigor to enterprise, and prosperity to the people. When its mission is accomplished, for which it went from the bank, it quietly returns through other channels to the bank to go forth subsequently carrying hope, life and activity.

If anything occurs to impede the circulation of the blood, if anything happens whereby each and every part of the physical body may not obtain all the blood required, sickness begins and death may be the result. If any cause prevents money from coming freely into the bank, whereby it can go out and circulate freely to any part of the country, sickness begins in commercial affairs, and death to the Nation may be the result.

In a study of circulation in the planetary system, juices in the plant, sap in the tree, water on the earth, blood in the body, and money through the avenues of commerce, we see that circulation is life, stagnation is death. Stop for an instant motion in the

planets, and chaos would result. Cease the flow of fluid
in the plant, and it withers. Prevent the circulation
of sap in the tree and the branches dry and the leaves
fall. Stop the flow of water and it becomes foul—
the earth parches and death to all living things is the
near result. Weaken the heart and the body dies.
Weaken the bank, stop the circulation of money, and
the prosperity of a Nation, resulting from its commercial activity, comes to a close.

Examine further, and we see that the power of
movement in the planetary system exists in the uni-
verse itself; so the power of circulation of the juices
belongs to the plant, to the tree, to the body; but
the power for circulating money that should belong
to the Nation does not belong to the Nation. It is
taken into the possession of individuals and so ma-
nipulated for their private profit, through the present
system of banking, as to impede the regular circulation with certain distress resulting in all the avenues
of business. The power of propulsion which gives
life to all that which we have mentioned, in order to
have healthy circulation, must belong to that with
which it is connected. This is evident in the fact that
the slightest deviation from regular circulation may
have very serious results. Prevent the usual evapora-
ation of ponds and swamps by tile draining, running
all the water rapidly out of a large area of country,
and drouth is the consequence. A slight cut may kill
the tree, a small derangement of the circulation of
the blood in the foot or the hand may cause death;
and the failure of a small bank in a distant state may
so derange the circulation of money in that region as
to precipitate a financial panic, causing general stag-

nation and distress in business throughout the country.

The lesson is that to secure health in earth life, in plant life, in physical life, in commercial life there must be absolutely regular circulation. This must come from a strong heart having the power to circulate the fluids, or the medium of exchange, through all parts of the body.

This leads up to an examination of our means of circulating money. Investigation shows that we have no means of uniform and regular distribution. Our Government determines what shall be money, stamps the value upon pieces of copper, nickel, silver, gold and paper, but makes no provision for ensuring circulation.

Nature provides a means whereby there is regular distribution of the fluids in the tree and in the body; but money, which is exactly analogous in its effect on commerce, to blood in the physical system, is left by the Nation to go whither it will according to the pleasure, the whim, the speculative tendencies, and the scheming manipulations of financiers.

Sometimes for a little period it will circulate freely and we are in an era of what is called good times. Again through the schemes and speculations of individuals it goes almost out of circulation to the sorrow and misery of large classes of people who are prospered by its free distribution.

It is seen by a study of the various circulating mediums which give health and life that quantity of that which circulates is not so important as regularity of distribution. Thus the person whose hands and feet are becoming cold cannot have health brought back by the injection of a large amount of more blood into the system. The quack doctor may suggest that as a remedy but the skilful physician administers a medicine calcu-lated to quicken the feeble action of the heart and re-store regular circulation.

As with the heart and the flow of blood, so with the distribution of money. If times are good at one por-tion of the year, when money is circulating freely, and hard at another portion of the same year, it is clearly not because of lack of quantity of money, but because of lack of distribution of money.

To propose, therefore, as a remedy for hard times, that a large additional amount of metal or paper money shall be brought into existence, when there are no means of circulating even that which is in existence, is like injecting a quart of blood into the man's arm, expecting a cure when the heart is so weak it cannot circulate the blood already in the system.

CHAPTER III.

This brings us to a consideration of the means by which money circulates. As stated before, money is the blood of commerce, the bank is the heart. Each is to the Nation what blood and the heart are to the physical system. The heart circulates blood, the bank circulates money. The only difference is that the heart and blood both belong to and are a part of the physical system. In monetary circulation, however, the money belongs to the people and the means of circulating it belongs to private individuals.

While the body, heart and blood all work in harmony, with uniformity of circulation, excellent health may be depended on, as long as the physical laws are obeyed. But not so with the people and the banks. To each other these are unfortunately in opposition. Like the buyer and the seller, each wants to get the most it is possible from the other. The depositor wants all the interest he can get from the bank. The bank generally insists upon paying no interest to the depositor, but exacts all the interest it is possible to obtain from the borrower.

The relation existing between the bank and the people is the same as would be illustrated by the physical body having possession of the blood, which is compelled to circulate through a heart which is separate and independent of the body; this heart being established as a blood-making enterprise for profit, the intention being to acquire all the blood it is possible to get from the body while the blood passes through the heart.

If the enterprise of establishing an independent heart is as successful as it proposes to be, the heart will come into the possession of all the blood in the body, and the body will have no blood left; or, if the heart does not get entire possession very soon, it can so manipulate the blood that it will not circulate; and thus it can make the body so sick that it will be glad to sell out to the heart for a small price. In any event the heart, being established as a blood-making enterprise, and all blood being compelled to pass through it, and the heart, having control of the law-making power, can so regulate matters as to get possession of all the blood.

If, in the endeavor to make blood for itself too rapidly, the heart should overdo the business, get out of order, and not send the blood which has been deposited in the heart back to the body, which yet owns some of the blood; and the body should lose confidence in the heart and refuse to deposit any more blood therein, but, on the contrary, should withdraw what blood it had in the heart and hide the same, then there would be great trouble because stoppage of entire circulation means certain death.

In this case the body is seen to be terribly sick

yet powerless.   It has lost confidence in the heart and
refuses to trust but very little of its blood to its
care. It has become panic-stricken and has hidden the
most of its blood wherever it can find lodging place.

The distressing effect of such withdrawal of circulation of blood from all parts of the body is at once
seen.   The result is a determination of the different
portions of the body, dependent upon regular circulation, to trample down all law and take blood wherever
they can find it.

This talk, which means anarchy and revolution, ex-
cites great fear in the feverish portions of the body
where the blood is.being hidden, the ultimate being a
compromise, fixed up between the ruling portions of
the body and the heart, by which blood is let out from
its hiding-place and allowed to circulate more freely
through the heart.

Through all this trouble the heart has laughed in
its sleeve.   It knew that the body had no means of
circulating blood except through itself.   Having had
all the opportunities for getting a large share of the
blood into its own possession, and being able to dic-
tate the law regulating its management, it could laugh
while it witnessed the distress and got big interest for
such blood as it furnished from time to time to the
starving portions of the body that required some
blood.

In this is seen the condition of the finances in this
country.   The people are the Nation—the body.   The
money which they possess is the blood.   The heart
is the bank: an institution which is established independent of the people for the purpose of absorbing and
getting into its own possession the people's money as

rapidly as possible. Through bad management and failure to pay back the money which is given the bank, the people have lost confidence. They have withdrawn their money from the bank and hidden it.

With the majority of bank owners this only causes a smile. They have the most of the money in their own possession. They know if ever money does circulate again it must pass through their hands, and they can get all the interest the law allows; and having large monied interests at stake they usually control legislation in manner such as to secure any law they want. Until money does freely circulate they can get this legal interest and a large commission besides, for money that they loan. Thus, it is all the same to them whether they loan much money at a lower rate of interest, or loan less at a higher rate.

CHAPTER IV.

In saying this there is no especial reason for ill-will to be expressed toward the present banks. Long before Christ drove out the money-changers in the Temple, the banker had been a necessity. As a means of circulating money, and the only means of regular money distribution, the bank is an indispensable institution to-day. That the managers of banks should protect their own interest through legislation, and otherwise, is to be expected. People in all other vocations do the same. Of that, therefore, we must not complain.

But that with which we may justly find fault is the relation which the banker holds to us. It is as if our cashier was acting independently of us and making all the money he could from us through his position, we paying him interest when we get money from him, he taking our money, giving us no security and no bond that he will return what he gets; he steadily taking in large quantities of our money, using it for speculation, unwisely loaning it, stealing it, becoming bankrupt and failing to return the money we give him; we losing all confidence in him, taking our money away from him and hiding it, and yet being obliged ultimately to bring it back to him because we have no other means of doing business.

To the ordinary observer this would seem to be a most unfortunate position in which to place ourselves, and yet this is the way we are situated in our relation to the bank. We place our money in the hands of our banker, who is interested in making money from us and not for us. Through heavy losses, by him, we lose confidence and we quit him. We hide our money; we stop business. We are finally starved out and have to come back to him. We make no law compelling him to do any better in the future. He stays right along. He laughs and continues to do business for all the profit he can get out of us. He knew we would have to return because we had no other alternative. He has a monopoly on all the profit there is in the circulation of money.

Why is this? Because we do not know any better. The banker is not to blame because we have no more intelligence. He finds the people without the facilities for the distribution of money. There is need of a custodian who will keep the people's money where the borrower can have access to it. He assumes the responsibility. We permit him to occupy the place. Surely the banker can not be blamed if the law is easy with him. It is not his business to pass more restrictions upon himself. And the people—well, when the time comes that money ceases to circulate and the times are hard, the dust is thrown in their eyes and their attention is diverted by other issues, one hobbyist filling their minds with the idea that the cause of hard times is an excessive tax placed on all goods in the shape of tariff.   Another individual is equally cer-tain that the cause of our distress is the probability that the tariff laws may be repealed.   A third is pos-itive that the refusal to purchase any more silver would be the salvation of the country.   Another is emphatic in his assertion that the free and unlimited purchase of silver bullion and the coinage of the same into silver money will save the country.   And so the contest goes forward, one calling the other a free sil-ver crank, the other retorting by pronouncing his op-ponent a goldbug.

Amidst all this dust, and fuss, and fume, about tariff, free-trade, gold reserve, free coinage, immigration, the Chinese, the sub-treasury and other issues, which are holding the attention of the masses, the banker is attending to his business, is proclaiming that money is very tight, is keeping as neutral as possible, while he gets big interest on what money he loans and is rapidly doubling his fortune through buying property, that has depreciated during the financial panic, at a quarter of the price which it will be worth when the panic blows over.

CHAPTER V.

Let us examine the force of these various arguments.
Suppose we have a high protective tariff? Admitted
that it will protect home industry and raise the rate
of wages; how can wages be paid and goods be bought
at the advanced price, if no money circulates?

Suppose we have free-trade, and goods can come
into the country from abroad in great abundance at
a cheap price; how can they be bought when there is
no opportunity to work and no money circulates?

Suppose we have free coinage and we increase the
quantity of silver money by a thousand million dollars,
how would the people get this money if we have no
means of circulation?

Suppose we shut out every Chinaman, every Po-
lander, and every Italian from coming into this country
in the future; how will that enrich the people now
here if we have no means of circulating money?

Suppose the sub-treasury scheme were to prevail and
farmers could borrow direct from the government, on
their produce as security, 80 per cent on its face value, at 2 per cent interest. What would very soon

become of this money if we have no means of circulation?

Free coinage, which is calculated to increase the
volume of money, and the sub-treasury plan designed
for the same object, it is thus seen would be of no
avail so long as we have no means of circulating this
increased amount of money.

The people should understand that their eyes are
simply blinded by the advance of these various issues
as remedies for the distressed conditions in business,
which prevail during the times of a financial panic.

There is another issue of vastly greater importance
for the people to consider, and that is, how to secure
regular and uniform circulation of the money already
in existence.

It should be understood that there are, at the present time, and all the time, hundreds of millions of
dollars hidden in safety depositories, in safes, stock-
ings and the people's pockets that do not have any
circulation, because they are thus hidden. This great
amount is vastly increased at times when banks are
failing in large numbers throughout the country. It is
then that the people become panic-stricken. They
fear they will lose their money if it is left in the bank
any longer and they go forthwith to get that which
they have deposited there. The money thus taken is
withdrawn from circulation.

Why is this money withdrawn? Because they fear
that the bank is unsafe. They lack confidence in the
institution from the fact that others have failed. They
fear this bank will go the same way. This may be
one of the soundest of institutions conducted by honest
and the best of bankers but the panic impels the de-

positors to make a run on the place in such great numbers, and so rapidly as to compel it to close its doors.

This failure adds volume to the wave of business trouble and the increasing flood carries down one bank after another, and one enterprise after another, until the land lies strewn with the wrecks of what might have been successful and prosperous but for the panic, begotten of lack of confidence in the banking institutions of the country.

Why this lack of confidence? Because banks fail. Why do banks fail? Because the system upon which they are conducted is at fault. To illustrate:

Anybody may open a bank. The owner, or owners, may be one person or more, may be honest or dishonest; no certificate of character is required.

There may be money in the bank and there may be no money placed there by the proprietors. The people are compelled to go to some bank anyway and this bank may secure their confidence to such an extent that one million dollars are there on deposit. The proprietors assume the responsibility of caring for this without giving one cent of security for it. This large amount of money, representing the hard toil of thousands of people, may be all lost and the proprietors of the bank not be held in the least responsible.

What an injustice! And yet the attention of the people is so occupied with other issues that they do not think of an expedient whereby they might be secured against the immense losses from bank failures which precipitate the financial panics of the country.

How the people are blinded! How the people are running wildly about the grounds crying fire, fire, without knowing where the smoke is coming from! Panic-stricken, in distress, and yet do not know the cause.

Stop a moment, friends, and think. Think: one minute of serious thought is often worth more than an hour of skurrying around in ignorance. The panic will sink the ship; ten minutes of careful planning may save it. Think.

Do you know that you feel safe concerning that greenback in your pocket? Do you have any anxiety about that postoffice order you have in your possession? Are you rushing over to the United States treasury to draw the money on that gold or silver certificate of deposit you have in your pocketbook? Not at all.

Why? Because you feel sure that it is as good as the gold. Why do you feel so sure?

Because the Government guarantees its payment.

The Government. Ah, the Government. You have perfect confidence in the Government? Of course you have. Every foot of land and penny's worth of property under the stars and stripes can be taxed for the support of the Government and the payment of its debts. You may well have confidence in the Government.

Would you run to draw your money from the bank if all its deposits were guaranteed by the Government?

Never. On the contrary, if you had any more money you would put it into the bank as the safest place wherein you could keep it.

CHAPTER VI.

THE PEOPLE OVERWHELMED WITH FINANCIAL TALK RELAT-
ING TO "SPECIE BASIS," "TEN-FORTYS," "BI-METALLISM,"
"OUTSTANDING CERTIFICATES," "FUNDING BONDS," AND
SUCH PHRASES AS INDUCE THEM TO THINK THAT FINANCE
AND BANKING ARE TOO GREAT FOR THEM TO UNDERSTAND
—THE SUBJECT VERY EASILY UNDERSTOOD.

Ah, here is a discovery. Let us enquire further.
We ask a thousand people—a hundred thousand—if
they would have perfect confidence in a bank guaranteed by the Government and they all answer in the
affirmative.

Here is a revelation. The wonder is, in a study of
Nature—in the perfect mechanism of the human system, heart and blood all belonging to the body, that
we could not have thought before that the bank holds
the same relation to the Nation that the heart does to
the body, and that the bank should belong to the Government, that all its deposits should be guaranteed by
the Government, and thus the bank be made absolutely
safe—confidence be restored and there be no more
withdrawal and hiding of money and no more financial
panic.

Can it be that this is all there is to the financial
question?

Yes, this is all. Do not let the politician fool you
with these outside issues that have nothing to do with

the finances and the circulation of money. Do not let
the banker confuse you with a quantity of high sound-
ing bank talk about "funding" the "five-twenties" into
the "ten-forties," "bi-metallism," "monometallism," gold
reserves," "clearing house certificates," and "currency
vouchers"—all calculated to convey the impression that
he is deeply versed in a knowledge of finance.

The facts are that while the banker is generally a
polished and an intelligent man his vocation has
never caused him to investigate a system of finance
that would be in the interest of the entire people. He
could not be expected to espouse a plan of finance
that would prevent him from getting all the money he
could in his occupation.   He is not following the business for his health. So far as his knowledge of finance
is concerned, it consists, of necessity, in information
about the reliability of individuals who may wish to
obtain money at his bank and the value of securities
which may be left by the borrower.

There is nothing very abstruse about the subject
of banking. It is not difficult to understand. The
bank is simply a place where we leave our money and
take no security. It is a place where we give security
and borrow other people's money if they have left it
there.   If the people do not leave their money at the
bank we do not borrow.

The banker gets a certain per cent for all the money
which he lends and herein lies his profit.

This is all there is to it. If the banker fails to return the money which we deposit we lose confidence
in banks in general. This universal loss of confidence
hides nearly all money and the result is stagnation in
business.

Anything that will inspire confidence—absolute confidence in the bank, will bring out all the hidden money and into the bank—any system of finance that will do that will add hundreds of millions of dollars to our volume of currency. and through regular circulation, the result of confidence, commercial prosperity will be assured.

We have seen that everybody will trust the bank that is guaranteed by the Government. It is clearly evident therefore, that all that is necessary then, is for the Government to guarantee the depositors that the money which shall be left at the bank shall be given to them when they ask for it.

The easiest method to accomplish that, will be for the Government to establish and own the bank.

CHAPTER VII.

"What! the Government own the banks and do the banking for the people? What plan would you suggest?"

"That the Government shall establish 3,000 banks evenly distributed at various central points in the United States, being at the rate of one bank for each 22,000 inhabitants.

"That there shall be 40,000 postmasters authorized to receive money from people on deposit in localities where there are no banks, which money so received by postmasters shall be sent to the bank to be loaned to those who may wish to borrow."

"How would you induce people who have long had their gold, silver and paper money hidden in places where it is now safe and easily accessible to them, to bring their money out from their safe hiding places?"

"We will allow them 3 per cent interest, per annum, on long time deposits. To the person who shall check out his deposits pretty frequently we will pay no interest, but to those who allow their money to remain in the bank, three or more months, without drawing upon it, we will pay interest."

"What do you think would be the total amount of deposits each year on which interest would have to be paid?"

"No one can tell that with any degree of certainty. A safe estimate would be $5,000,000,000."

"And the interest on that amount at 3 per cent would be $150,000,000 annually?"

"Yes."

"And your 40,000 postmasters, what are you going to pay them?"

"We will allow them, each $2,000 per annum, making a total of $80,000,000 to postmasters each year for collection of moneys from the people in the back districts. Thus you see like the rivulet that runs to the brook, the brook to the river and the river to the ocean, so the smallest driblets of money will be gathered into the loaning depositories to be in readiness for use by those who wish to borrow."

"Yes, true, but your banks, what are you going to pay them for doing the business?"

"We will pay them liberally and as follows:

To 1 President per year....................$ 8,000
 " 1 Cashier............................... 5,000
 " 3 Appraisers each $3,000................ 9,000
 " 4 Assistant Appraisers, each $2,500..... 10,000
 " 4 bookkeepers, each 2,000............... 8,000
 " 4 Assistant bookkeepers, 1,200.......... 4,800
 " 10 clerks, each 1,000................... 10,000
 " Miscellaneous 5,200
             Total $60,000.

Banks, of course, in some localities might require a larger force, in other places the number of clerks might be less."

' "Is not this a very large amount of money to be paid for the conducting of the banking system of the country in behalf of the people? Let us see the figures representing the total cost to the Government of conducting its own banking."

"Very well; here you have them:

Interest on $5,000,000,000 of deposits at
  3 per cent per annum................ $150,000,000
Salaries of 40,000 postmasters at $2,000
  each............................ 80,000,000
Expense of conducting 3,000 banks at
  $60,000 each........................ 180,000,000
                                     _____

Total annual expense of conducting the
  banking........................... $410,000,000

"Four hundred and ten millions of expense in conducting the banking system of the country. How could the Government pay its expenses were it to take control of the banks?"

"Very easily indeed, and have an immense profit besides. If it is legitimate for the Government to accept of revenue from imports, spirits, tobacco, the sale of postage stamps and money-orders, it would be equally legitimate to accept revenue for the use of money which might be loaned. Were the Government to establish its 3,000 banks as a depository for all the money in the country it is safe to presume that nearly all the money in the country would come into these banks."

"How much money have we in the United States?"

"According to the United States Treasury report of 1892 there were in the hands of the people, $1,600,000,000 which were known to be in banks and in general circulation.   At a very low estimate there are $400,000,000 of money hidden; thus making $2,000,-000,000 which would come almost immediately into the Government banks to be loaned.   This distributed among the 3,000 banks gives each about $670,000 as a capital with which to begin operations. This money is all in readiness to begin banking with—no new money would have to be made for this purpose because checks here serve as money.   This system proposes to do banking in the same manner that the banker now does business; take the people's money on deposit and loan it to customers who wish to borrow."

"What interest would you charge?"

"We would make a uniform interest charge in all parts of the United States of 4 per cent per annum."

"You have only $2,000,000,000 to loan, the interest on which would be only $80,000,000. This out of your $410,000,000 would leave you behind in your running expenses $330,000,000."

"Ah yes, apparently so; but do not go so fast in your estimate. We shall employ the best of banking talent to manage the Government banks and we propose to do as the successful banker does to-day—loan this money over and over.

"Thus, for illustration, a bank of the present time has 1,000 customers, and $10,000 in the bank.   We will suppose it is a prosperous year; there is no financial panic abroad, everything is moving smoothly in finance and the bank has the complete confidence of the people.

"Jones borrows $1,000; pays it to Smith who deposits it in the bank. This money is now ready to be loaned to Brown who pays it to Snow, who deposits it in the bank. The bank pays nothing on its short time deposits but charges, say, seven per cent as interest to the borrowers. In a short time that money has been loaned out ten times to as many customers, each paying seven per cent, which is 70 per cent interest, or $700 for the use of that $1,000 one year; and if business is moving along smoothly, and nobody is taking out and hiding his money, the amount of deposit will just about equal the amount which is borrowed, so that the $10,000 in the bank in the beginning is there at the end of the year.

"This is the way bankers make their great fortunes. Not by loaning money once, but by loaning deposits over and over.

"Thus see the report of one of the large National banks. Capital stock, $1,000,000. Deposits, $20,000,-000. Loans $15,000,000. They pay no interest on that $15,000,000 of deposits but they get, on the average, 6 per cent per annum interest on the $15,000,-000 of loans. Figure the profit to that bank on loaning $15,000,000 which has not cost the bank a cent of interest. Profit to the bank in twelve months, $900,-000. That is the reason why bank shares of $100 in some popular banks are worth from $300 to $1,800 each; because there is such enormous profit in banking—getting the people's money for nothing and loaning it at a good, round interest.

"Under Government ownership of banks we propose to be much more liberal. We are going to give the people the advantage of its benefits from the very first.

In the beginning we estimate, in paying 3 per cent on time deposits, that we will distribute among the people $150,000,000 annually in interest. Following this we propose to reduce the average rate of interest throughout the United States one half, by charging only four per cent per annum.

"On chattel mortgages, poor people, who cannot afford it, are paying from 20 to 60 per cent per annum throughout the entire land. In the middle states, on the best of landed security, interest rules at from 6 to 8 per cent, besides a commission to the money broker, of two or three per cent, for his trouble in finding the money. Throughout the Northwest the interest rates run from 8 to 12 per cent and a commission besides.

"An unfortunate fact about this is that, even with the best of security, the poorer the people the more interest they have to pay. John Smith who is well situated down in Massachusetts can get money at 5 per cent. His brother James, who has been unfortunate in business, in his effort to begin again, settles with his family on a farm in Dakota. All seems bright before him until he finds his profits cut off by a 12 per cent interest. This is an outrage and everybody ought to see it.

"With cyclones, hurricanes and grasshoppers devastating the lands, with drouth and low prices making the profits uncertain, the 8 and 12 per cent interest plaster has been steadily at work, summer and winter, the farmer and his family denying themselves all the common enjoyments of life in order to pay this interest and retain possession of their little properties.

"Nothing has so greatly retarded the Northwest, in its development, as an exorbitant interest which has con-

tinually settled, like a dark cloud, over the face of the
entire country. We propose to reduce the rates of
interest to 4 per cent, through Government control of
banks, making it possible for James Smith, on good
security, to borrow money in Dakota as cheaply as
his brother John does in Massachusetts. He buys
postage stamps and money orders as cheaply as his
brother does, why should he not get his money as
cheaply?

"Why? Yes; why? Simply because the people of this
country have allowed the financial legislation to be
controlled by a set of men who were interested in the
loaning of money for their own personal profit.

"We propose to change this condition of affairs by
placing the rate of interest at a uniform standard of
4 per cent."

"Yes. Well, please tell us how you are going to
pay your expenses of $410,000,000 per year, which is
the cost of conducting the banking of the country?"

"We can show you very easily and how we will
make an enormous profit besides. We shall have $2,-
000,000,000 immediately deposited in our banks by
the people. We will loan this over and over, as it is
borrowed and deposited, again and again. During
the year, at a very low estimate, it will be loaned over
ten times, so that the amount of money we shall loan
will be $20,000,000,000. The interest on that sum is
$800,000,000. We subtract $410,000,000 from that
and we have left, as a clean profit, $390,000,000 per
annum."

CHAPTER VIII.

HOW WE WOULD BORROW FROM A GOVERNMENT BANK—
BANK OFFICIAL NO LONGER COLD AND AUSTERE—ONLY
WISHES TO KNOW WHAT SECURITY WE HAVE TO OFFER—
PLENTY OF MONEY—ANYBODY CAN BORROW ON GOOD SE-
CURITY—NO PARTIALITY SHOWN BECAUSE THE INDIVID-
UAL IS RICH OR A CUSTOMER OF THE BANK—NO MONEY
TAKEN FROM BANKS—BUSINESS DONE WITH CHECKS—
THE BENEFITS ARISING FROM THIS SYSTEM.

"That seems all right. Tell us in detail how an individual would borrow money if he went to a Government bank"

"We will suppose John Doe wishes to borrow $1,-000. He applies to the cashier of the nearest Government bank, stating the amount he wishes to borrow. Doe will be immediately impressed with the difference in manner between this gentleman and the cashier of the old bank. The latter was cold and taciturn, his reply almost invariably being that money was "very tight," were only loaning to their "own customers," etc., etc., as much as to say. "Be a customer of ours if you want or expect to borrow money." If a loan was made the customer was made distinctly to understand that a great favor had been bestowed.

Under the new conditions the cashier simply asks Doe where his security is. Upon being informed, an appraiser is at once dispatched to make examination.

This security may be real estate or personal property. In either case it must be free from incumbrance, insured against fire and all accident, and in such condition that it will sell, at forced sale, for $2,000, or twice the amount which Doe wishes to borrow.

The security being found all right the appraiser returns and informs the cashier that he can safely loan Doe $1,000 on the proposed security. The necessary papers are quickly made out, the Government having all abstracts of title brought down to date, and Doe gets the money—a straight $1,000 without having to pay a commission of $30 to a broker for finding the money and from $50 to $300 to an abstract maker."

"What does Doe do with this money?"

"He turns around before leaving the bank and deposits this thousand dollars and takes a check-book to draw checks against it, as he may require. He expects no interest on his deposit as he is going to soon draw his money out on checks, but he pays 4 per cent per annum."

"What next becomes of that money which Doe deposits?"

"It is in the bank ready to be loaned again, as it is in any bank to-day when people deposit money. In the course of an hour Roe comes in, wants $1,000, gives security, gets the money and deposits the same before leaving. Having an absolutely safe bank in which to deposit there is no object in carrying money in the pocket when checks will pay all debts and make purchases just as well as money. During the day ten persons borrow that $1,000, and nobody takes the money out of the bank. The same amount of money that was there in the bank in the morning is there at night. Twenty thousand dollars' worth of value has been turned over to the bank as security, the bank has gotten 40 per cent, or $400 for the use of that $1,000 per year, in the process of loaning it over and over, and the circulating medium, through these check-books, that has gone out, has been increased $10,000. *This increase in amount of currency, which so many people clamor for, comes in these checks which may be made a legal tender for all debts."*

"This seems possible. What would you claim are the principal benefits of the system?"

"We cannot enumerate in an hour all the benefits, but you will recognize the following:

" I. Absolute safety of the bank as a place for depositing money.

" II.   Relief from anxiety to all persons who deposit money in the banks.

"III.   The inducement for the common people to acquire and save money that they may place it in the bank and get 3 per cent interest on their deposits.

"IV.   The constant abundance of money in the bank by which any person can always borrow who has security.

" V.   The absolute impartiality by which the poor can borrow as cheaply as the rich, the man in Idaho borrow as cheaply as the man in New York.

"VI. Freedom from broken banks, which precipitate the financial panic, which shut down business, which starves out the laboring man, which compels the poor to sell for what they can get in order to have something to eat.

"VII.   Freedom from the hard times, resulting from bank failures, in which period the rich take advantage of the poor, who are out of work, to buy that which they are compelled to sell at a quarter of the value.

"VIII. Freedom from the distressed conditions from time to time in which the millionaire so rapidly doubles and trebles his fortune.

"IX. The abolition of the chattel mortgage shark that gets his 5 per cent a month when banks are failing and money is hidden.

"X. The abolition of the money broker who gets his living through the simple finding of places where money can be borrowed during the continual period of hard times.

"XI. The settled financial conditions by which people can know what to depend upon when they engage in business.

"XII. The immense revenue to the Government of $390,000,000 per year—a clear profit over and above all present means of revenue.

"XIII. Freedom from the expense borne by people who pay annually hundreds of thousands of dollars to safe manufacturers and the proprietors of safety depositories for the custody of money in these hiding places.

"XIV. The convenience and safety from robbery of doing business with checks instead of being compelled to carry and use money in all business. transactions.

"XV. The low rate of interest to borrowers by which the money expended in interest can be saved and put into general circulation instead of going into rich money loaner's hands at the great financial centers."

CHAPTER IX.

'Please explain how the poor man is benefited by Government ownership of banks."

"That is easily done. The great majority of borrowers who pay an enormous interest are poor men. The low rate and saving of interest to them, is so much money gained.

"The poor man, who has three hundred dollars' worth of furniture, if he borrows upon the same one hundred dollars, will pay an interest of four per cent per month on the average. That is $48 for the use of that $100 per year. If the Government appraiser finds that that furniture will actually sell for $200 the borrower can get the $100 and pay therefor, as interest, $4 per year instead of $48.

"The average farmer in the West will find his interest lowered one half by this system. Supposing his interest is $400 per year. He saves by the new system $200 per annum. In ten years that is $2,000. With that he builds a new house. That means men, now standing in idleness, to fell the trees in the for-

est, more workmen required in the sash, door and
blind factories, in the brick-yards, in the stone-quar-
ries, men engaged in the manufacture of hardware,
paints, oils, glass, furniture, mechanics in carpentry,
masonry, painting, plumbing and glazing."

"See how business begins to revive and the idle get
employment, through the farmer saving $200 a year by
having to pay only 4 per cent interest."

"The immense impetus given to enterprises of every
kind, through a lowering of interest, it is impossible
to estimate. One of the first questions asked by the
experienced business man is whether the profits of
the enterprise, about to be entered upon, will pay the
interest. If in doubt the work is not commenced and
the workman does not get employment."

"How is interest continually kept so high at the
present time?"

"There are two reasons for it. One is that the continual hiding of money by people, who have no confidence in banks, causes money always to be scarce.
This is the more plainly seen during the time of a
financial panic, when banks are failing. At that time
money is almost universally hidden, and so scarce in
circulation that any one having it to lend becomes an object of veneration; while the money he has
to loan commands a very high price. Another reason for
high interest, besides bank failures, lies in the political influence of bankers in our State legislatures."

"What can the banker do there?"

"You introduce a bill into the legislature, for the
purpose of lowering the rate of interest, and see what
he can and will do. Immediately a lobby in the
banking interest, composed of lawyers, ex-members of

the legislature and others, supposed to have influence with the legislature, appears at the Capitol for the purpose of convincing the members of the legislature that the proposed reduction in the rates will drive all the money out of the state. This argument generally prevails and the legislature adjourns, to the relief of the bankers, without disturbing the existing rates.

"People who have never studied finance have little idea of the effect on the profits of banking by the lowering of interest even one per cent. Suppose there are ten large banks in a metropolitan city. On the process of loaning over and over, their loans during the year, will amount to a hundred millions. By taking off one per cent their profits are reduced one million. That is one hundred thousand dollars for each bank; a very nice plum and they never want to lose it. It is thus easily seen why they have their agents in the body of the legislature and in the lobby when there is any probability of a lowering of the rates of interest.

"Of course we cannot blame bankers for their course of action with the legislature. The people are never wise enough to think of the benefit arising to the community by a saving of one per cent interest, whereas to the banker it is a matter of vital account. It is their duty to look after their own interests. The farmer does that when he resorts to law to protect himself against oleomargarine or disease in cattle, and the banker should be expected to do the same thing."

"But may not high interest be beneficial? Is it not a fact that times are better when money is greatly in demand and commands a good rate of interest?"

"There are times when there is such probability of

land, in certain localities, or of certain commodities
becoming very scarce, that the circumstances might
warrant the payment of a greater interest in order to
secure the same; but with the intense competition
continually going forward and prices tending down-
ward, the profits are not sufficient to warrant the payment of large interest of late years in any line of industry.   Many men having learned that fact, have sold
out their business and gone into the sole business of
lending money.   All the smaller villages and cities of
the country have their quiet sitters around who are
doing nothing but warming dry goods boxes and holding down chairs in some neighboring store while they
watch their interest money.   In order to get large interest and justify themselves in taking it they get in
the habit of croaking about the times.

"To these individuals a bank failure and a financial
panic are a God send. It enables them to get big interest and say "I told you so."   Were interest rates lowered to a reasonable figure, and to a point where there
would be less profit in lending money, these individuals would bestir themselves into some productive
employment where they would be of service to the
world, while using their capital in some enterprise
that would give work to others."

CHAPTER X.

"If it is well to lower interest why not stop interest entirely and do business for cost?"

"Because to place the rates of interest any lower than we have here proposed—that is 3 per cent on time deposits and 4 per cent on loans—to set the figure any lower would destroy values and create too great a change in business. To illustrate:

"Tens of thousands of aged and infirm people, minor children and widows are living off the proceeds of interest money loaned at 5, 6 and 7 per cent. To bring the rate down to even 3 per cent, which would become the rate on long time deposits, is an enormous reduction which is liable to bring inconvenience to many people who have made their arrangements and settlements on the basis of a higher interest than that. All the insurance companies are making rates on the basis of loaning their money at 5 per cent and upward. Were the rates to come down to 3 per cent and they be able to get no more than that on the money they loan, the reduction will be all they can endure. To place the rate below 3 per cent would be simply to send them into bankruptcy."

"Any discussion of a system of finance which would immediately put the rates of interest down to two or one per cent will meet with so much opposition, from the hundreds of thousands of persons who are interested in getting a larger interest, as to cause any such system to fail of adoption."

"Why can you expect to establish a rate of 3 per cent on deposits and 4 per cent on loans? How can you expect to have friends enough to carry such a measure through?"

"Because those rates are high enough to immediately fit into present methods of doing business without creating any great shock in the financial world. Bankers, stockholders in successful banks and all money loaners will, of course, oppose it; but we shall have on our side, at once, all money borrowers, as these individuals will favor any system by which they can always find money at the bank, and be able to borrow it at a rate as low as 4 per cent.

"We shall at once have the great masses of the common people on our side, all those who wish to and expect to deposit money in the banks and want to get as high as 3 per cent interest on their deposits.

"Whatever may be the abstract right of a principle it is folly for a political party, any organization or person, to take up and advocate an idea which, while possessing some of the elements of right, they cannot carry to a successful issue.

"In the days when letter postage was 25 cents, it was clearly right that the postage should be only 2 cents, but it would have been folly to have forced the issue at that time, of an immediate reduction to 2 cents.   It is better to start in the direction of right and get there as rapidly as possible.

"The enormous profit of loaning money by the Government at 4 per cent per annum, and the large surplus coming into the treasury through this source, our managers of finance may think after a while should be given back to the people in the shape of lower and lower interest.   The inference is that the time may come when the banking of the country will be conducted for cost.   But ample opportunity should be given before that for the business relations of the country to adjust themselves to this condition."

"While we are discussing the subject of interest let us have your opinion on the question of moral right to take interest.   We have a large number of people who consider the taking of interest an extortion. What is your opinion upon that subject?"

"We may have abstract ideas of right which it is impossible to enforce.   It would seem to be the privilege of any people living anywhere upon earth to go to any other part of the earth.   But the law of self protection, living as we do in this competitive age, may require that we deny certain people the right to come among us. It would seem just that goods manufactured in any part of the world should be shipped into another country free of duty.   And yet for the protection of home industry the managers of the Nation's affairs may deem it best to impose a tax on all such goods coming from abroad.

"We must take conditions as we find them and govern ourselves accordingly.   To say that there shall be no interest is to say that no rent should be paid and no compensation shall be allowed for anything that we use.   To illustrate:

"Jones owns a farm, under a high state of cultivation, supplied with buildings and conveniences which he has made by labor.   Failing health or other reason may cause him to withdraw from the farm. Knowing the place to be vacant an individual comes forward who is very willing and anxious to rent the same and pay therefor $300 per year.   The tenant can pay that and have left a handsome profit besides.

"The rent thus received supports Jones and his family in his declining years when he is no longer able to work.   In due time the tenant proposes to purchase this farm with its improvements and does so, paying therefor, $10,000.   This money which comes into the possession of Jones, through the sale of his farm, he loans at 3 per cent per annum, the total yield in interest being $300 per year.

"Surely if it was right for Jones to rent his farm and receive as compensation $300, it is equally right for him to rent the proceeds of the farm for $300.

"It is simply for Jones to determine which way is the most convenient for him to get $300 per annum as his means of support.

"Any political party having a financial plank in its platform, which places the rate of interest very low or abolishes it altogether, may advocate a right in the abstract, but in this hard, undeveloped world, where labor, land and money require compensation, for use, it is difficult for this party to convince a great number of people that business should or could be done any other way.   Such a party may do great work

through agitation, in educating the people to a com-
prehension of better and more exalted ideas.   But as
conditions are not yet ripe for the adoption of their
views, they must be content to advocate what they
deem best and leave other parties to assume the management and make the laws for the people.

"We say this in justification of the position we have
assumed in Government ownership of banks, that the
rate of interest should be as high as 3 per cent on
long time deposits in order to do justice and satisfy
the masses of the people, and the Government banks
should not be expected to loan at less than 4 per cent
in the beginning."

CHAPTER XI.

"Does the Government ownership of banks offer other advantages than what you have here mentioned?"

"Yes, it can easily be the means of putting a stop to all petty thefts, all danger of being slugged by the highway robbers after dark, will stop all house-breaking, all burglary, all murder for money, all holding-up of stages and railroad trains. It will dispense with the necesssity of two-thirds of the present police force in all cities, it will empty the police courts and the jails and will turn over the penitentiaries to other uses.

"In fact it will make the facilities for detecting and capturing a thief so absolutely certain that the thief is compelled to quit the business."

"These are very broad assertions and very important if you can prove it. What are your grounds for such a belief?"

"These may seem like very strong statements but you will very soon agree that this may all be true.

"The passage of all banks into Government ownership makes the bank an absolutely safe place for money so long as the Government shall endure. It is the safest place in the country in which to place money. It is so safe that all persons will use the bank, and all money may be and probably all money in the country will be kept there.

"If all money is in the bank it cannot be lost, burned or stolen."

"But how are we to do business without any money on the person or about the house?"

"That is what we were about to tell you. Your money is in the bank. Your bank-book shows how much you have there, how fast and when you deposit.

"You want to use money. You may do as the average business man does to-day, receive from the bank a book of blank checks and when any bill is to be paid, pay the same by a check drawn upon the bank."

"Yes; very true. But I want to buy and pay for a newspaper, want to pay car-fare, want to buy a railroad ticket, want to pay my hotel bill, one thousand miles from this point two days from this time, and while in that city I wish to travel by street railway, by ferry, and by private conveyance, want to visit places of amusement, and patronize, every day, a dozen enterprises and institutions that will require money in amounts all the way up from one penny to five or ten dollars. How am I to do that without money?"

"You will do that very easily when we tell you. Did you ever see the specimens of postal currency in denominations of 5, 10, 25 and 50 cents, which the

United States government issued at the time of the late war?"

"Yes."

"Those slips of paper served their purpose admirably. It was very much more convenient to carry ten dollars in that kind of change than to carry silver. It was considered a great improvement over silver and the people went back to metal with regret and have often requested the Government to issue some kind of fractional currency since then that would be as convenient to use as that was.

"The only objection to it was that which applies to the old bank bill to-day. It became dirty, smutty, foul, and filled with the scent and disease of the vile and filthy person that carried it. That is the objection at the present time to a paper money, that is carried in all sorts of pockets, by all sorts of persons, absorbing often a contagious disease from being held close to all sorts of bodies.

"We are now going to tell you of something better —vastly better even than that postal currency.

"You are about to go upon a journey. You want to pay all debts, make all purchases, and yet carry no money. To do this you apply at your nearest bank—the bank where you do business—or the bank where you are known—for a coupon check-book, for illustration, worth $500. You pay something extra to have this book prepared, especially for your convenience. In the meantime you give the bank officials your photograph, your method of signing your name, and they take an accurate measurement of all parts of your body together with a full personal description of yourself.

"In a few days you receive your check-book with a private stamp to be used in stamping all your checks before you pass them. The book is a small oblong that goes easily into the side pocket and is bound in such a cover—either leather or other material, as you have ordered.

"You open this book. On the first page is your photograph, a memorandum of the measurements of your body, a copy of your signature, an impression of your stamp, together with the seal and certificate of the justice, that you, the bearer of this book, are John Doe, of the town of ——, County of ——, State of ——, engaged in the business of ——, are—— years of age and these are your measurements, photograph, signature and descriptions of your personal appearance, the original duplicate of which is in the bank for future reference when required.

"All this is upon the first page and is not to be torn off or used, but is specially to be kept, like a passport of a traveler in a foreign country, for the purpose of identification.

"You open further into the book and find checks of all denominations from one cent to ten dollars. On each check is your portrait, finely engraved, your signature, the measurements of your body, the impress of your stamp, and the denomination of your check.

Each check is easily detached, by means of perforations, from a stub having a corresponding denomination upon the same, so that you may know, if you knew in the morning, by your stubs, how much you have expended during the day, if you examine your stubs at night.

"There are one dollar's worth of one cent checks in

your book, two dollars of five-cent checks, five dollars of ten-cent checks, ten dollars of twenty-five-cent checks, twenty dollars of fifty-cent checks and so on; a quantity of one-dollar, two-dollar, five and ten-dollar checks, in amount up to five hundred dollars.

"This check-book is good for five hundred dollars when the checks are stamped by the owner upon the back. Until they are so stampèd they are only worth so much paper."

"How will we use those checks?"

"We will suppose you start this afternoon on a long journey, but before going you have considerable business to transact. You will buy a newspaper, will purchase a guide, will buy a trunk and a new hat, besides getting a railroad ticket. In anticipation of what you are to use, you stamp a number of your checks and tear them out of your book as you have occasion to use them."

"Will everybody take these checks readily?"

"Certainly. Why not? As soon as people get used to the system they will take them as readily as they used to take postal currency. Will take them as willingly as we now take bank bills, never looking or caring about the bank they are on.

"What, buy newspapers with checks?"

"Certainly; as soon as the newsboy discovers that he can handle these one-cent, two-cent, five and ten-cent checks as easily, the checks being of different colors according to different denominations, the boys will handle these checks as readily as they do pennies."

"Yes, but what will the boy do with these checks? He cannot pass them to any one else for money, can he?"

"No, he will not need to pass them for money. Should he take in two dollars and a half to-day, or a quarter of that amount, or less, he will pass them into the bank in exchange for his own check-book which may be filled entirely with one-cent, two-cent and five-cent checks, and while these may not have his portrait upon them, they will serve the purpose, with his stamp upon them, he being able to make his purchases with these and make change with them."

"Too complicated. Too much fuss for a' little business. Don't think the people would take to this system. Would prefer pennies, nickels and silver."

"Yes, that may be, and there will be nothing to prevent small transactions being carried on with silver and small metallic change. It will be possible, however, to put all the money in the bank and do business entirely with checks, good only when they are stamped if people so desire."

"Do you say that you could buy your trunk and your railroad ticket with these checks?"

"Yes, certainly. After merchants and ticket agents become accustomed to this method of doing business, it would be very easy."

"Would these checks pass in distant cities?"

"There is no reason why they should not. The traveler, one thousand miles from home, in settling his bill of seven dollars and fifty cents at the hotel, would tear off a five-dollar check, a two-dollar check, and a fifty-cent check, would turn them over, and after stamping upon the back, if not already stamped before, would pass them to the hotel clerk. If any doubt should arise as to identity, he has but to step into the office and have his measurements taken. If

they correspond with the measurements indicated upon his check, no doubt can exist as to his identity."

"What does the landlord of the hotel do with the
checks that come in from all the patrons of the hotel
to-day?"

"He endorses each one with his own stamp and the
entire amount, received to-day, being a hundred,
five hundred, or a thousand dollars, he deposits in the
bank to his credit.   Each check is returned to the
place where they were originally issued.

"The landlord does not pass these checks out again
as money.   He simply deposits them to his credit.
Thus, for the thousand dollars received from travelers,
the bank will give the landlord a thousand dollars,
either as money or checks with which he pays all his
obligations.

"As is the case to-day among business men, checks
received would not be passed to others, but they would
be endorsed and deposited in the bank to the credit
of the depositor, everybody in the purchase of articles
or the payment of obligations using their own checks."

"Then you would use no money at all according to
this system?"

"No, checks take the place of and represent money
which is in the bank. You would use a check-book and
either write in the amount you want to pay, as business people do nowadays, or use a check-book filled
with checks of all denominations, your only trouble
being to stamp the back of the checks. If you did
not want to stamp the checks at the time you passed
them you could stamp them all at your convenience
and thus they would be always in readiness for use."

"It seems to me that you have a cumbersome system that the people will not accept."

"It may seem so at first. But this is all there is to it. In a neat little book you have fine slips of paper of all denominations. When you want to purchase anything you tear out one of these slips of the denomination you require. In another small book you will keep all the checks you receive. Those you receive you will deposit any day in the bank, just as you now deposit checks, postal money orders, or money. The only difference between the checks you thus receive and money, being that when you deposit your checks you will stamp each one. Of course before going to the bank you could stamp all your checks in a minute just as you now endorse postal money orders and checks before you pass them into the bank, or you can stamp them at the bank. It would not take over two minutes to stamp hundreds of dollars' worth of such checks as you would be likely to receive."

"But suppose I lose my check-book?"

"Well, now, you see the advantage of this system. If you lose your pocketbook with your money, you are liable to never receive it back, but in the loss of the check-book you would notify the bank of your loss, giving a description of the amount of unused checks. You would get another book and pay for it. Watch would then be kept of the checks that came from your other check-book. If you had not stamped your checks nobody would attempt to pass them. But whoever may pass them will be compelled to endorse them, and that endorsement will capture the person who stole your check-book or found it and attempts to use it without the right to do so.

"Of check-book No. 21, dated July 1, for $100, which you lost, only ten dollars' worth of checks came into the

bank. The bank will therefore return you $90. Thus
you see you never can lose one dollar by fire, theft or
any other way, when the Government bank is established in all parts of the country, and everybody's
money is in the bank."

"You say that the person to whom money is paid
will be compelled to stamp the check before it is deposited in the bank, and suppose the person who pays
out money does not wish his banker to know where
his money goes, what will you do with the person who
will not do business thus with checks?"

"Please understand that this check system is optional
and not imperative. The individual may demand from
the bank gold, silver or paper money, such as we have
now and pay the same as we do now. Or he may do
his business mostly with checks and carry a little silver with which to make small purchases and make
change. The system, however, permits of doing business wholly with checks in a manner such that money
cannot be lost by thievery.

"When the system comes into general use and nobody carries money, then the pickpocket quits business, the burglar leaves his profession, and the high-
wayman bids farewell to the road. For the first time
in the history of this world, civilization has devised
a plan that outwits the thief, and he is compelled to
quit the business of stealing money because there is
none in the people's pockets, none in the people's
homes, and none being transported from one portion
of the country to another by express companies or
any other way."

"How would the banks escape the necessity for
transporting their money from one portion of the country to another as they do now?"

"The bank in any portion of the United States would receive the money on deposit from all the people living in that vicinity. That would be a sufficient capital with which to do business, especially as no one would ever take money from the bank, but, as a rule, would do business with checks which serve the purpose of money."

"How would I send ten thousand dollars to Hiram Wilder, Palace Hotel, San Francisco, California, by this new system?

"You would simply deposit that amount in your bank and give the name and address of the person to whom you wished that amount paid. The officials of the bank would then send word to their bank nearest to the Palace Hotel to give Hiram Wilder ten thousand dollars when he proves his identity. You would write or telegraph him to call for his money.

Under this system of Government banks, established in all parts of the country, there would be no more of this crude method of doing business, in carrying money from one part of the country to another, making a temptation to train wreckers and highway robbers."

"You said in the beginning of this talk about checks that you could prevent stealing."

"Yes, we can stop stealing absolutely as a profession. To stop it as a profession will pretty nearly abolish it completely."

"A thief could steal my watch, or my horse, could he not?"

"Yes, but he would not unless he intended to sell the watch or the horse."

"Why could he not sell them?"

"He could, but when he sold them he would take checks in payment. In order to pass the check he must be identified."

"Suppose he is identified, how will that capture him? Suppose William Wiggins steals my watch and the next day sells the same to Abraham Solomon. He offers Solomon's check at the bank, is identified as William Wiggins and gets the money. How can we fasten the stealing of the watch on Wiggins?"

"Very easily. Solomon is a pawnbroker. The law compels each pawnbroker to send in the number of each watch purchased by him to the headquarters of the police station. You leave a description of your watch at police headquarters and your watch is traced to Solomon's. At this place you learn that he gave a fifteen-dollar check for the watch. An order is served on Solomon compelling him to turn over the check when it is returned to him through the bank. In due time the check comes in endorsed by William Wiggins. It now takes but a brief time to capture Wiggins.

"Under the present system we have no means of knowing who stole the watch and never will know. With the aid of the new system, through the means of checks, which the law might make compulsory with pawnbrokers, we capture the thief in a brief time. In fact, detection is so absolutely sure, if the thief sells what he has stolen, as to make his arrest and punishment a certainty. This makes stealing so dangerous as to oblige the thief to quit the business. Occasionally, only occasionally, a thief will steal an article for his own use, but that is very seldom. He almost invariably steals money or something that can be readily sold for money."

"Why not introduce the check system at the present
time if by this means we can stop all stealing?"

"Because the people will not generally put their
money into the banks sufficiently to carry the plan into effect. To-day people suspect the banks. They
lack confidence in them.   They will not trust them.
Consequently they carry their money upon their persons, or have it hidden somewhere about their homes.
This makes the continual temptation to assault, rob,
and if necessary, kill.

"Everybody's life is in danger because of the present system of banking. Change the banking system
from the present insecure, uncertain, unreliable method of banking for private profit, to Government ownership of banks, and everybody's money would go into
the bank, where it would be safe from bank failure, and
the depredations of pickpockets, burglars and highwaymen. Continue the present system of allowing
private individuals and private corporations, under the
guise of "National" banks, to swindle and rob the
people for their own individual profit, and the people
will so distrust all banks that they will keep their
money out of these institutions and in places where
thieves can get access to it. Under these circumstances, the pickpocket will ply his trade, the desper-
ado will make every journey after dark and in lonely
places an uncertainty, the burglar will fill every home
with anxiety, and the traveler may expect at any minute that his train will be thrown from the rails or held
up by highwaymen for the purpose of robbery.

"Continue the present system of banking, allow ir-
responsible men without bond or restrictions of any
kind to continue the custodians of the people's mon-

ey, compel people, through lack of confidence in these men and these banks, to hide their money in all sorts of places, and you not only make it forever scarce but you create such inducement to thievery, you scatter temptation so broadly, and you manufacture thieves so fast as to necessitate a constantly heavier tax upon the people in the support of a large police force, the management of criminal courts, the maintenance of criminals in the county jails, and the constantly growing, greatly increased number of long term criminals in the State prisons of the country.

"Change the system of banking—bring it all under the control and ownership of the Government, inspire confidence so that people will put all their money into the banks—and you not only make money permanently abundant thereby, but in making it impossible to steal without detection you at once suppress all that species of crime, save life and property from devastation, exempt the people from taxation for criminal proceedings, empty the jails and penitentiaries of their inmates, and prevent all that species of crime which is the terror of society in all parts of the world."

"Can it be possible that all this reform could be effected by simply changing the banking conditions?"

"Certainly. Carefully examine the subject for yourself. Make banks safe. Put all money into them. Do business only by checks or some small change in silver if you prefer, and we have made the greatest advance in civilization ever accomplished in any epoch of the world's history."

CHAPTER XII.

SECURITY THAT SHALL BE GIVEN WHEN WE BORROW AT GOVERNMENT BANKS—AMOUNT THAT CAN BE BORROWED ON REAL ESTATE OR PERSONAL PROPERTY—$500 PER CAPITA IN CIRCULATION—IS THIS A SYSTEM OF WILD INFLATION OR IS IT NOT?

"You speak of making money permanently abundant by this system. It is generally understood to be necessary that we shall keep miners constantly at work, getting out the gold and silver bullion, the mint steadily at work in converting this into coin, while the Government printing presses are at work turning out greenbacks. How do you propose to avoid this?"

"As explained before, by establishing 3,000 banks, giving a population of 22,000 to each bank, we shall bring into each bank about $800,000 of the money already known to be in existence. As shown also before when money is borrowed it will not be taken from the bank as it is now. The bank being the safest place in which to keep money all that is borrowed is immediately deposited and a check-book representing the amount of money which is deposited takes the place of the money in circulation."

"Instead of gold, silver and greenbacks, you have checks wholly for circulation?"

"Yes. Business is largely done that way now. That idea is nothing new. With the Government ownership of banks business will be almost wholly done that way. When the people become accustomed to the ease and simplicity of doing business by simply tearing off a little slip of paper, the system will become as universal as the use of postage stamps, in fact will be much more common, as all moneyed transactions will be done that way."

"How great an amount of checks can come into circulation that way?"

"That will depend upon how much money people borrow. If checks are used to represent the money in the banks there will be about two billion dollars worth of checks, making about $32 per capita in circulation. But that can be greatly expanded. Thus a conservative and safe rule, in lending money, is to loan one dollar on two dollars' worth of actual wealth that will sell at that rate at forced sale.

"The individual having twenty thousand dollars' worth of property, that will sell under the hammer for that amount, should be entitled to borrow $10,000 on that amount. Having borrowed and deposited that amount he would have the privilege of putting ten thousand dollars' worth of checks into circulation which would be the same as so much money in the transaction of business.

"Thus the amount of money which any person can put into circulation will depend upon his amount of wealth, he being able to borrow an amount of money equal to one half its worth. This rule would apply to the people in any community. If the actual and bona fide wealth of any town is one million dollars, according to the most careful and conservative assessment, then that town would be entitled to borrow five hundred thousand dollars on the entire property of that town as security. This is an entirely safe and conservative view to be taken of financial matters. If for any reason the outlook for the town should be uncertain, so that property values would be uncertain, and the total property would not sell for over one hundred thousand dollars, then the highest amount that could be borrowed would be fifty thousand dollars. The time of loan on all property, both personal and real estate, should be on sufficiently short time, also, as to permit of no depreciation in value. Frequent appraisement of property would be safest for the Government."

"On this system of circulation, based upon actual wealth in the country, how much money could there be per person in the United States?"

"By the census of 1890 the total wealth of the country was shown to be $62,000,000,000 or $1,000 per person. At that rate we could borrow $31,000,000,-000, which divided among our population of 62,000,000 of people, would give us $500 per capita of actual cir-culation that we would be entitled to and could have."

"Five hundred dollars per capita! Why that would be inflation of the wildest kind, would it not?"

"Not at all. To illustrate: Suppose Jones wants to borrow $1,000. He offers real estate or property of any kind that will sell, in the dullest of times, at forced sale for $2,000. He should and will be able to obtain $1,000 on that security. There would be no inflation in that. The loan is borrowed on actual value, so insured against loss by fire, wind, flood, death or any other cause, that there could be no pos-sibility of loss as business is done to-day.

"This circulation would be based on actual value.

Such a circulation, when it is assessed by very conservative and cautious men, could not be considered as
inflated.   On the contrary it would be the soundest
money system in the world, as every dollar in circulation by individuals would be based on actual value
passed over to the Government when money is borrowed; which securities could be sold at any time
when the borrower did not promptly pay his debts.

Think of it, with all the struggle of certain parties
to make the quantity of money in the country to be
$50 per capita in circulation, and here it is shown
that by Government ownership of banks and all circulation based on actual value in the possession of the
people, the circulation may be rightfully $500 per
capita."

CHAPTER XIII.

UNDER GOVERNMENT OWNERSHIP OF BANKS WHAT USE
WOULD THERE BE FOR GOLD?—WHAT SHALL BE DONE
WITH SILVER?—SILVER AS A MONEY—WHAT IS THE FU-
TURE OF SILVER?

"What do you propose to do with gold in this system of banking which you offer?"

"It is seen, that doing business with bank checks very largely, a metallic currency, especially gold, would not be indispensable in the transaction of business, except that gold would be in demand in foreign exchange. The bank being opened by the Government and all deposits guaranteed, it is probable that tens of millions of dollars in gold, now hidden, would come into the banks for the purpose of getting the three per cent interest on long time deposits. Gold would therefore be much more abundantly in sight than it is now. If any change were to take place in gold it would be lower in value than it is at present

"Required in foreign exchange and more and more in the arts, mining for gold will, of course, go forward as vigorously as now."

"Would not the free and abundant coinage of silver prevent financial stringency at all times?"

"No money can be devised that will permit a ready circulation, at all times, with the present system of banking. With confidence destroyed in the bank, money will be hoarded and, though the volume of silver dollars should be increased a hundred fold, it would be easy to hide all this increased amount of silver.

"A great increase in volume of money is not so necessary, it is seen, as that we have the means of ready circulation of that which we have.

"As a large share of the population will not submit to doing business with checks, silver must be coined to supply their demand. With the increase of population the use of silver coin will continue actively in use as a money, in what proportion of volume it is impossible to say, as no means exist of telling now how much silver might be used by the people, in proportion to checks, if they could get it freely.

"It should be understood that whatever the volume of silver which may be coined and issued, it cannot do great and good service if silver, or silver certificates, are hidden, through people having no confidence in the banks."

CHAPTER XVI.

PROFIT TO THE GOVERNMENT, $390,000,000 PER YEAR FROM DOING ITS OWN BANKING—HOW THIS MONEY SHALL BE EXPENDED—FLOODS AND DROUTHS POSITIVELY ABOLISHED AND PROBABLY CYCLONES—$100,000,000 ANNUALLY SET APART FOR THIS PURPOSE—AN ARMY OF MEN EMPLOYED—THE COUNTRY IMMENSELY ENRICHED—PRODUCTIVE POWER OF THE SOIL GREATLY INCREASED.

"You claim that under Government ownership of banks there will be a profit of three hundred and ninety millions of dollars each year. Would it not be well to give that to the people in the shape of lowered interest, as we have benefited the people by lowering the rates of postage from twenty-five to two cents?"

"We have before stated that the very rapid lowering of interest would work great injury to people and corporations who have made investments, made contracts and adjusted their affairs for some years to come on the present rates of interest. It would be ruinous to a large class of people to lower rates too rapidly. We doubt if it would be wisdom for the Government to reduce rates below four per cent for some years."

"What then will you do with this large surplus of money?"

"Evidently it would be wisdom to expend it in the giving of employment as widely as possible, on public improvements, which will carry the greatest amount of blessing to the people.   Three hundred and ninety millions a year!   We will use one hundred millions of that amount annually during the next ten years for the purpose of abolishing floods, drouth, cyclones and wind storms in this country.   Whether we can certainly stamp out cyclones or not, you will agree with us that we can suppress floods, with all their accompanying loss of life and millions of dollars' worth of damage, and we can prevent drouth.

"To accomplish this, of the 2,400 counties in the United States, we will select 2,000 that need our assistance.   One hundred million dollars appropriated to them will give $50,000 to each.

"We first begin with a study of the cause of floods. We find by examination, that tens of thousands of miles of tile drainage have been scattered over this country, from two to three feet beneath the surface of the soil, which drains have been run through thousands of the sloughs and lowlands of the country that formerly held water in storage for several months. Not only do these drains afford opportunity for the water in the lowlands to depart quickly, but the great amount of tiling on the uplands permits the outflow of water, from all parts of the country to the streams and to the larger rivers, with great rapidity.

"Thus the heavy rains falling in the up-country carries with it, through the tile drain, the mud of the newly ploughed ground, the dirt and the debris of the fields, in hasty flood, to the great rivers like the Ohio and the Mississippi.   There, in their slower movement, the mud, held in solution, gradually settles to the bottom, raising the bed of these rivers, so that an equal amount of water will overflow the banks next year more

easily than they do this. Along with the steady ele-
vating of the beds of these rivers, other hundreds of
miles of tile drains, all pointing outward towards the
streams, are being laid each year, so that the outflow
of water will be more and more rapid each succeeding
season. Thus it is easily seen why the flood becomes
greater and more devastating each year.

"With this understanding of the cause of floods we
begin the work of their extinction. We place at each
county-seat a Government commissioner who, with fifty
thousand dollars in hand, offers, $500 to any person
who will construct a lake, covering an area of one acre
or more, three feet in depth, and turn the tile drainage so that the water, of that vicinity, at the time of
rainfall, shall all run into this lake.

"This proposition when carried out, will give to
each county one hundred lakes during each year, and
one thousand lakes to each county during the next ten
years.

"It is easily seen in this that small lakes, thus constructed, while ornamental and serving the purpose
for boating, raising of fish, and production of ice, can
be made in sufficient number, in conjunction with dams
in the streams, to hold all the rainfall, and thus effec-
tually prevent the flood.

"The water, thus held during the hot days of summer, will evaporate, and the moisture, thus passing into
the air, will so come back in dews and rains as to prevent the drouth.

Think! throughout the arid plains of the great west,
where, for long periods of the year there is no certainty
of rainfall or any living vegetation, all will be changed
by the construction of reservoirs of water by which there

will be a certainty of moisture and good crops. Think
how immensely this will add to the prospetity and
the wealth of the people, while giving employment to
the great army of men engaged in the construction of
this important internal improvement."

"Yes; that is true and that is right.   But about the
cyclone.   How are you going to prevent that?'

"The suppression of the cyclone will come along
with the abolition of drouth. The denuding of the land
of water by the tile drain, and the cutting off the forest
have made such large areas of dry, hot air, as to
generate great quantities of electricity in the atmosphere.   It only requires the coming together of
two currents of air, of different temperature, to start the
super-heated air into a whirling motion, when, electricity being generated, rapid rotary movement gathers in fury, and devastates everything that comes in its
path.   The moist coolness of the atmosphere, the result of wide-spread evaporation, from the tens of thousands of lakes, regularly scattered over the country, will
so change the condition of the air as to prevent the
cyclone and probably the frequent lightning."

"That rather seems probable and may be true.
What about the suppression of winds that often occur
in the midst of rains?"

"The hurricane is the result of another cause, but
comes also largely from drouth.   Over a large extent
of country, where there is but little water, the sun
shines warm for days and possibly for weeks.   Over
all that expanse, of possibly hundreds of square miles,
the air is heated and expanded.   Then comes a rain
that quickly cools and so contracts the air where it
falls as to leave what may be termed a hole in the

atmosphere. The vacuum thus made in the hot air, by
the sudden cooling, has to be filled, and the air rapidly
rushes toward this place from all directions."

"Possibly the rain has extended over a large area of
a hundred or two hundred miles square. The contraction of air leaves an enormous space, requiring air
to fill the same from far distant regions outside this
area where it is raining, and the rush of air is for the
purpose of filling the space made vacant by the cold
rain."

"The universal distribution of lakes as reservoirs of
water, over the entire country, will cause such general
evaporation of moisture as will cool the air and prevent this sudden contraction of atmosphere, which results from the heated, expanded condition of the air,
over a large area of dry ground."

"A severe wind may sweep with resistless fury for
scores of miles across a sheet of water and we wonder
why it blows so. The cause, is in the passage of air,
possibly at a great distance from the storm, across water and land, for hundreds of miles it may be, to fill
the vacuum made by heavy rain over a large area of
hot and dry country."

"This severe wind will be removed by the wide
distribution and evaporation of water over the entire
country."

"It is even possible, that we may escape the severely
cold north winds of the winter and the extra heavy
tax for fuel by preventing the sudden atmospheric
changes in the Southern states, in the winter time,
which occur over large areas of dry country. Thus a
cold rain at a period of warm weather, in the South,
will so condense the hot air as to make a great vacuum;

to fill which the air from the North will be called upon to move in that direction ; and hence the cold north
wind steadily bearing down upon us to fill the space
made vacant by the condensation of atmosphere in the
South. A steady even evaporation of moisture over
all the otherwise arid regions might prevent this."

"Very well. There may be something in that.
We will not take up time now to dispute it. We want
further light. Would not the waters in the numerous
lakes which you propose become stagnant and un-
healthy?"

"No. The author of this work, in 1886, made just
such a small lake, as here described, near his residence,
at Glen Ellyn, Ill. Where rests this sheet of water,
over an area of about two acres, was a swamp which
was only a disfigurement to the farm. Out of the ex-
cavation, for this lake, came the fertilizing material
that so enriched the surrounding ground, as to give
three crops of hay each year. The water, agitated by
every passing breeze, is more pure than that which
lies dormant in any well or cistern. This body of
water is stocked with fish, including carp and gold
fish, and, aside from being an ornament and a pleasure, is a source of profit in its supply of fresh water
in summer and clear ice for the entire year."

"What will you do with the remainder of your profits
in banking? You have left yet two hundred and
ninety millions of dollars for annual expenditure."

CHAPTER XV.

OF THE $390,000,000 IN ANNUAL PROFIT FROM GOVERNMENT
BANKING, $100,000,000 TO BE EXPENDED EACH YEAR ·
IN THE MAKING OF GOOD ROADS——80 MILES OF SHADE
TREES SET AND 40 MILES OF SUPERIOR ROADWAYS CON-
STRUCTED IN EACH COUNTY PER YEAR—THE BOY OF TO-
DAY, WHILE YET A YOUNG MAN, MAY SEE EVERY ROAD A
SUPERIOR DRIVEWAY AND EVERY COUNTY IN THE POSSES-
SION OF 1,500 MILES OF DELIGHTFUL SHADE-TREE FOR-
EST.

"We will take another hundred millions and give annually fifty thousand dollars to each of the two thousand counties in the United States that ought to have
better roads.

"We will appropriate one thousand dollars to the mile
to be expended upon those roads first that have the
most travel.   Of this we will use two hundred dollars
in the setting of elm trees upon each side of the roadway, six hundred we will use for grading and tiling,
where the water might otherwise stand, and two hundred dollars, besides some local taxation, possibly, we
will use for continual scraping and smoothing of the
surface, thus keeping the road in permanently good
order.   Each year we will add to the county about
forty miles of good roadway.   In ten years we shall
have four hundred miles, and in twenty years eight
hundred miles of superb roads, delightfully shaded

in summer and breaking the force of severe winds in winter. Estimating that we have 1,500 miles of drive-way on the average, in each county, it will not be many years before we have the entire number of roadways improved by this source of revenue, and easy, communication effected, whereby the letter carrier can reach every farmhouse.

"With the bicycle abroad the demand has become imperative for better roads. With the necessity existing for more frequent intercourse among people in the rural districts good roads must come. How will they come?

"At present the only means by which they will come will be by a burdensome tax imposed upon the people. Through Government ownership of banks the profits of banking may be such as to give us superior driveways, delightfully shaded all over this country, furnishing employment to an army of workmen and no tax therefore imposed upon the people. Trees set and roads made under scientific supervision, would be as different from the hodge-podge mud roads now under the control of ignorant local roadmasters as light is superior to darkness."

"Yes, very true; this is good. You have employed great numbers of heretofore idle men and you have certainly made a wise expenditure of one hundred million dollars a year in making superb roads and stringing over each county 1,500 miles of forest, conferring the great benefit which attends the setting of trees. What will you do with the one hundred and ninety millions yet left in your possession?"

We make no further suggestions as to expenditures. Time will reveal how this income can best be used.

CHAPTER XVI.

CORRUPTION IN POLITICS ABOLISHED — GAMBLING AND THE SOCIAL EVIL SUPPRESSED—BANKING AND THE CIRCULATION OF MONEY INDEPENDENT OF PARTY CONTROL—THE FUTURE AND THE PRESENT BANKER.

"How will Government ownership of banks affect the corruption existing in politics, the continual tendency toward gambling and the social evil?"

"We have shown before how the great and continual abundance of money in the banks and the ability to obtain it at a low rate of interest, will start enterprise of every description into being. The saving in interest will permit hundreds of thousands of farmers to improve their conditions by the erection of better buildings. This alone will revive nearly all the industries. This will be followed by demands for labor in every employment.

This abundance of money, readily obtained on good security at a low interest, together with the annual expenditure of three hundred millions of dollars, in carrying forward public improvements, will give such full and free opportunity for everybody to get employment as to enable the seeker, now after office, to get a living without holding office; it will enable the gambler to get a certainty of support instead of risking his all in games of chance; it will enable the criminal to find employment so readily, when he leaves his prison, that

77

he will not be forced to commit crime again in order
to maintain existence; and it will provide work in such
continual abundance for young men that they can see
a steady support for themselves and family in the future.   In that event they will marry.

"It is not necessary to go into a very lengthy argument to prove that prosperous financial conditions,
whereby all can have continuous employment and all
participate in the Nation's prosperity, will dispose of
political corruption, the thirst for gambling and the
social evil.   Give us Government ownership of banks,
restored confidence in finance, and even circulation of
money, and we have so thoroughly abolished the conditions which produce crime as to allow the clergyman
to picture for his congregation a brighter outlook and
shorten his sermon one-half."

"Will not the moneyed affairs of the country come
thus under the control of one party that will become
all powerful?   How can you prevent that?"

"In each Congressional district we will elect five
bank commissioners at a separate election, this election
being entirely non-political. These commissioners will
have control of the employment of bank officials.
Each commissioner will hold office for two years,
may be eligible to re-election, and may be continued in
office so long as financial affairs are in healthy condition in that district.   Should money be improperly
loaned and the banks suffer losses by reason of incom-
petent officials, the bank commissioners would be held
responsible, and by the people directly, and not by
the appointing or removing power of any party. Thus
these commissioners could be removed and others selected to take their places by direct vote of the people.

The office should of course, be entirely non-partisan."

"What will you do with the present bankers?"

"Remember, when perfect confidence exists in the bank and everybody can get some interest if they allow their money to remain in the bank a certain length of time; when everybody is saving money and even children are depositing in the banks; when all business is being done with silver money or new, bright checks, which like the railroad ticket is used but once or twice; when nearly the entire adult population, and a large proportion of the youth, are using the banks, there will be a great demand for bankers. The service of every banker of to-day and five times as many more will be in immediate demand. All will have employment."

"Yes, but you cannot get the best business talent at such a salary as you would be willing to pay. How can you secure the best banking skill for the Government service?"

"We do not require, under the new system, as much skill as is now necessary. To-day the lending of money, on the security which is given, is so much a matter of chance as to require a great deal of judgment on the part of the banker. Under Government ownership of banks, however, the rule will be to loan money only on actual property, which must be worth, at forced sale, twice the amount which is borrowed. It thus becomes simply a matter of appraisement, requiring the judgment of a good assessor.

"The skillful banker of to-day, should he not wish to engage in Government employ as a banker, will find plenty of opportunity, in the universal flow of money, for acquiring wealth in other enterprises. He

and his leading stockholders are money makers. Given
the free opportunity to acquire and they will accumulate as rapidly, in other enterprises, as in banking."

"There are many honest men doing a good business
in various kinds of vocations who now get accommoda-
tions at the banks without any security other than
their reputation.   What shall be done for these?"

"Under Government ownership of banks, all loans
requiring absolute security to be given, there would
doubtless spring up numerous guarantee companies,
which, for a small consideration would guarantee a
borrower at the bank.   Or these borrowers could secure
the endorsement of some friend, who has continual security at the bank, which is perpetually held to enable
the individual to get money whenever he wants it,
up to a certain amount.

"Thus no reason exists why money cannot be obtained by any one as easily as now and, unlike conditions existing at present, any person, whether rich or
poor, a member of any organization or not, a patron
of the bank or not, a friend of the cashier or not—any
person having absolute security, real or personal, can
borrow at a uniform rate of four per cent interest,
whether the security is upon the widow's furniture or the
millionaire's real estate, whether the borrower lives in
the wilds of Idaho or on Fifth Avenue in New York."

CHAPTER XVII.

GOVERNMENT OWNERSHIP OF BANKS, RAILROADS, ETC. —
CIVILIZATION TRENDS TOWARDS CO-OPERATION—LOYALTY
TO A GOVERNMENT SECURED BY MAKING A PEOPLE PART
OWNERS OF THE BANKS—THE OLD UNITED STATES BANK.

"What do you think about the Government taking
so much upon its hands, as the ownership of telegraphs, railroads and banks. Is there not too much
paternalism in all this?"

"The difference between individualism and paternalism is the difference between bearing the burden alone,
and bearing it together. It is true that it takes a
higher civilization to co-operate in harmony, than to
transact the business alone. The most savage wild
beasts, like the tiger, hunt alone. The less savage,
like the bison, giraffe and elephant go in companies.
Man, in the savage state, is alone. As he becomes
more highly civilized he gathers into the tribe, becomes a part of the town, the county, the state and
the Nation.

It has taken a century to change the John Smith
store into the John Smith Company store. So it will
be in the ownership of public properties. It costs a
great deal of money to buy the telegraph and the
railroads, but as other nations have purchased from
private companies their railway properties to the
advantage of the people, so it is probable our country

will some day absorb these public conveniences. But, unlike those expensive properties that require an immense tax to be levied in order to buy them, the establishment of the Government bank requires practically no expenditure whatever. It is only necessary to open a room and the people will do the rest. The money comes in immediately and the bank, like the banker of to-day, proceeds to do business and make money on other people's money."

"Although Government ownership of telegraphs and railroads is important, the ownership of banks is infinitely more important to the people, as upon the regular and uniform flow of money hangs the commercial life of the Nation. The employés may quarrel and dicker with the managers of railroad corporations and the people will switch round by another route and go on with their business, but when banks become unreliable people lose confidence and business comes to a standstill."

"But suppose the Government had absolute control of all the money in the country, gold and all being in the banks and suppose a war comes on?"

"In that case woe to the party that makes war upon this Nation. Where the treasure is the heart is. If you want a loyal people you want their money to be at stake."

"Had the people of the Nation had all their money in the Government banks at the opening of the late war there would have been no war. As it was, a large share of the people had no interest in the financial success of the Union, hence the disloyalty. Make the people part owners in the financial system of the country and you make them truly loyal and invincible against the foreign foe. In reality, though all money would be in the Government banks, every depositor would be as free as he is to-day to draw out his money, convert it to other uses or with his money go to any other country. Should the Government require money to carry forward a war or any enterprise strictly governmental in character it would borrow money as it does now. It would not confiscate depositors' money in the banks."

"It seems as if you had a pretty strong case. It certainly is right in theory and it would seem that we ought to carry it out in practice. Why is it that this has never been thought of before?"

"From the fact that the thinking upon this subject, and the legislation upon this subject, has been left to those who were interested in the perpetuity of private banking for private profit.

"From the fact that it always has been so the common people have supposed that it must be so.

"The great bulk of the common people are averse to thinking. They prefer to follow in the old rut. Ask a Chinaman why he shaves his head—His forefathers did it. Ask the spruce coachman in top-boots and cockade, why the bridles on the horses' heads carry great blinders that almost obscure the animals' eyesight—He will look at you in amazement. He never thought of it. Ask the people why they are willing the profits, arising from banking with the people's money, should go into the hands of millionaire bankers in Europe and America—and they too will look at you in amazement. They suppose it must be so. They never thought upon this subject. "

"Has there never been any attempt at Government ownership of banks?"

"Yes; and always with benefit to the people. The postal savings banks of England and the money order system of this country are steps along that direction. Though a private institution and conducted for private gain, the appointing of Government directors to assist the other directors in the management of the Bank of England has been a large source of strength to that bank. The manufacture of the greenbacks and the guaranteeing of the bills by the United States Government has given us the best money we have ever had."

"What about the Old United States Bank? Was that a government institution, and if so why did it fail?"

"The first bank of note in this country was the Bank of North America, established in 1775, during the war of the Revolution, for the purpose of raising money to carry on the war. This bank proposed to raise two millions of dollars, but went forward in the issuing of paper promises to pay until it had distributed three hundred million dollars in continental currency, which having no value behind it, became valueless.

"The next bank was the First Bank of the United States which was established in 1791, the capital to be ten million dollars, divided into 25,000 shares of $400 each. Corporations and individuals might be subscribers to the stock and the Government might subscribe to the extent of $2,000,000. The renewal of the charter of this bank was defeated by the casting vote of Vice-President DeWitt Clinton and the institution wound up its affairs and went out of existence in 1811. This was evidently a private institution run for private profit, the Government being a part owner.

It proved to have been successfully managed and yielded a profit to the stockholders.

"The second United States bank was organized in 1816. Capital $35,000,000, of which $7,000,000 was to be subscribed by the government and $28,000,000, in shares of $100 each, by the people.

'It was prohibited from lending more than $500,000 to the United States, more than $50,000 to any state, and to any foreign prince or power whatever, without the sanction of law obtained therefor. The bank commenced business in 1817, its charter extending to 1836. At the time its charter was obtained specie payment had been suspended throughout the country. When this bank was opened confidence was so restored that specie payments were resumed in all the banks and the country had a prosperous financial era extending for several years. The bank was essentially a private institution, however, being conducted for private profit under the wing of the United States Government. The bank grew to be a strong political power, through the private interests that governed it, and it finally began to be feared. A desperate effort was made to obtain a recharter of the institution but owing to a veto of a bill for recharter, on alleged constitutional grounds, by Andrew Jackson, the bank went out of existence as a United States Bank in 1836.

CHAPTER XVIII.

"How would this new proposed Government ownership of banks differ from the old Bank of North America, the Old United States Bank, the Argentine Republic monetary system and other financial schemes
that we have heard of?

"It is unlike those systems of finance in that all
money loaned must be upon values, worth, at forced
sale, twice the amount of that which is borrowed.

"A system of money is said to be inflated where
there is not a sufficient value to redeem it. An individual having property worth, under the hammer,
$200 could safely give his note for $100 because he
can pay the note and it is not probable that the property, worth $200, will so depreciate in value that it
will not be worth $100."

"Should the individual give his note for $200 it
would be liable to discount as there might be some
risk that he could not sell his property for $200 and
redeem the note. Should he give his note for $400
with only $100 worth of security, it would be imme-
diately subject to a discount of 50 per cent unless he
was known to be honest and was doing a prosperous

86

business. Even that would not prevent depreciation.

"As with a person so with a township or a Nation. A town containing assessable, taxable property worth $1,000,000 could safely give its note for $500,000 if the appraisement was based on very careful, conservative judgment as to the future prospects of the town. To bond the town for $1,000,000 or more when property, for various reasons, is liable to depreciate would be hazardous and the notes (or bonds as we call them) would be liable to sell in the market at a reduction from their face value.

"At the time of the Revolution, the entire population excluding Indians and slaves, was only about 3,000,000, and these people were all greatly impoverished by the war. The continental money was issued in amount up to $300,000,000. As it was impossible for the property of the people to pay that sum, the only alternative of the people was to repudiate the debt."

"What was the difficulty with the Argentine Republic?"

"It was this: With an estimated population of only 3,900,000, three-fourths of whom are Italians, one-tenth Spaniards, one-twelfth French, and the remainder other nationalities, with an annual revenue of $73,-000,000 and a yearly expenditure of $92,000,000, in 1890, with a National debt of $475,000,000—with this small population and large debt, the government authorities issued, in 1891, and converted the same into paper money, the large sum of $300,000,000. With the evident inability to pay these notes their paper money so depreciated in value that it was only worth 27½ cents on the dollar.

"Prominent bankers in London, having great faith in the Argentine Republic, had taken these bonds at a much higher valuation than they were actually worth, and when they so went down in value, it caused great losses to financiers in London and resulted in the financial panic that soon spread over England and Australia and reached the United States in 1893.

"The issuing of so much money on the small population and uncertain securities of the country was rank inflation. The individual having $100 of property would be equally justified in giving his notes for $400, getting the money and expecting this money to pass current for the full value of $400. This might go for a time, but as the individual's resources became known, there would be depreciation in value of that money, it becoming worth no more than 25 cents on the dollar."

"What is meant by inflation, and inflated prices?"

"When the individual can pay his note in anything that has actual value, his note is not inflated. When he has obtained four times as much money by his notes as he can redeem, his money is inflated. The Argentine Republic had issued three times more money than they could redeem in actual value. Money was plenty, goods became scarce, prices rose to correspond with the abundance of paper money. Thus an article the year before worth 30 cents became, with the abundance of money, worth 90 cents in paper money. We thus see inflated money and inflated prices. The Old Continental money was inflated and as long as it circulated there were inflated prices. When it disappeared goods declined in price to a gold standard."

"Did we not have inflation during our late war?"

"There was really no inflation as the country always had sufficient property to pay debts in gold, but the great amount of greenback dollars in excess of gold dollars at one time made it seem as if there was inflation. Hundreds of thousands of men went from the productive industries into the ranks of consumers. Goods became scarce. Everybody had confidence in banks. All money came from its hiding-places, went actively into circulation, and being more abundant than goods, goods rose in value, and prices seemed to be inflated. When the war was over, however, the soldiers returned to the work of producing, and having made a great abundance of goods, even more than sufficient to supply the demand, prices went down."

"What is the difference between the goldbugs and the greenbackers?"

"The first has always contended that no more paper money should be issued in this country than could be redeemed in gold. When confidence exists in the banks and all the money is in active circulation, both paper and metallic currency, money is abundant and times are said to be good. When the people lose confidence in the banks money becomes scarce, through the hiding of money.

"During the panic of 1873 banks failed, people lost confidence and money became scarce through its being hidden. It was then that the greenback party was organized, their claim being that the Government should issue enough greenbacks to make times easy, giving as security the general resources of the country, regardless of whether there was a sufficiency of gold in the country to redeem all the paper money that was issued or not.

"The goldbugs, as the greenbackers term them, have opposed this financial system on the ground that if one Congress should conclude to issue $1,000,000,000 in excess of what is now in circulation, prices of all kinds would be inflated or increased over 30 per cent, and that nothing would be gained as it would take just so much more money to buy anything, the only advantage to anybody being that the person who was in debt could pay the debt easier by the inflated currency. They further claim that, according to the whim of any Congress, inflation might go up and up, until some succeeding Congress might conclude to curtail, when prices would fall."

"Well now, please explain how your system differs from the goldbugs and the greenbackers."

"Yes; having explained the other systems ours may now perhaps be the more easily understood by comparison.

"In the first place we claim that there is no need of making or issuing any more money; that there is a sufficiency now in the country with which to do business—money that we have been steadily accumulating for the past 400 years, money in great abundance. But owing to lack of confidence in banks this money is hidden.

"We further claim that were we to double the amount of money we have, or treble or quadruple it, such great increase of volume of money would not benefit us in the least as it would be just as easy to hide four times more money than to hide what we do now.

"With this plain understanding of the subject we advocate first, that there be a system of banking whereby we may freely circulate money. To that end we demand that the Government take the custody and loaning of the people's money into its own hands, for the purpose of securing the confidence of the people and bringing all the money now in the country into circulation.

"In loaning money we are as conservative as the most zealous gold advocate can require. In lending money—say one hundred or one thousand dollars, we demand security that will sell at forced sale for twice the amount, in gold, that is borrowed. We say gold because this metal being a recognized standard of value, people know what we mean.

"What system can be more safe? If we have loaned $100 we should be able, and our system is wholly based on the idea that we can sell our security for $200, standard gold value.

"We loan readily to any one who will bring us that proportion of security, and we loan any amount that may be required. What more can the greenbackers ask? Our circulation is based on the resources of the country and no whim of Congress could inflate or contract. Like the healthy man whose blood circulates with regularity, all that would be necessary in monetary managment would be for financial quacks, hereafter, to let the patient alone."

"How would Government ownership of banks affect our public debts?"

"It would have nothing to do with it. It is wholly a separate matter from the issuing of bonds by which the Government borrows money."

"What would become of the present Government bonds?"

"People would draw interest upon them at 3 per cent per annum as they would upon their long time deposits in the bank. Gradually, as the Government prospers, the bonds will all be paid while the Government gets out of debt."

"What do the Government bonds have to do with National bank circulation?"

"The plan pursued has been for the Government to borrow money of bankers and give its notes, called 'bonds.' These bonds, which draw interest and are to be paid by the Government when they mature, are placed in the custody of the United States treasurer at Washington.

"With these securities placed at Washington, the banker has been allowed to issue national bank notes up to the full amount of the bonds which he had deposited less ten per cent. Thus if he deposits $100,000 in bonds he can issue $90,000 in bank notes.

"The deposit of these bonds and the printing of the bills by the Government makes the bank-bill of to-day absolutely sound. The bills, however, do not serve their purpose because lack of confidence in the banks causes people to hide them, from the fear that should they give these bills back to the bank, as a deposit, they may lose them.

"The proposition made by some financiers for Government to issue more bonds to the bankers, in order that they may issue more paper money, it is seen would not overcome financial stringency because the distrust of banks will continue so long as banks fail, and however great the additional amount of national bank-notes which may be put out, such added volume would avail nothing so long as they would not be circulated."

CHAPTER XIX.

THE GOVERNMENT SIMPLY A CUSTODIAN—PEOPLE FURNISH
ALL THE MONEY IN GOVERNMENT OWNERSHIP OF BANKS
—STRAIGHT BANKING—GOVERNMENT RECEIVING A SMALL
COMMISSION ON ALL LOANS—A HAPPY PEOPLE; ALL EM-
PLOYED—MONEY EVENLY DISTRIBUTED —A PEACEFUL,
HIGHLY PROSPERED NATION—HOW TO INAUGURATE THE
SYSTEM.

"Does the Government involve itself in any way through the banking system you propose?"

"Not in the least, other than the care which is assumed when we take the charge and management of any enterprise. The Government furnishes no money. For the sake of inspiring confidence it simply becomes the custodian of the people's money and gets a small commission for doing the work. The commission though small, is large in the aggregate.

"This banking system we propose is for the common good of all. That is easily seen and understood. It is not established as a money-making institution, though, as we have seen, loaning money at 4 per cent yields a large revenue to the Government.

"The bank we propose requires no Government issue of money, like the Argentine Republic, or the proposed Sub-treasury scheme, by which the Government is to issue money, ignore all other money, and loan directly to the people.

"The system we propose is simply to do business as the bankers do business to-day: open banks for the people in which to deposit their money. The Government being responsible for the safe keeping of the same, confidence is thereby restored, the bank fills with the people's money—good substantial money that has been honestly earned. This money the Government bank will loan, as the banker to-day loans the people's money, and receives a commission for handling the money, which is as legitimate as for the Government to receive a revenue on the manufacture of any article, or when goods are imported into this country from a foreign nation.

"The Government does a straight banking business, but as it issues no money except greenbacks, coin and checks, which will be legal tender, in exchange for money deposited, there is no opportunity for inflation."

"Do you mean to allow other banks to do business?"

"As all banks which are conducted for private gain, in their eagerness to do business and make profit, are liable to so manage affairs as to derange circulation, the public policy, as is the case with private postoffices, would require their suppression. A tax might be imposed upon private banking, as was done upon the state bank issues for the sake of the National banks, which would drive private banking out of existence. We do not quibble, however, on that subject. We have no war to make on any of the financial issues that agitate the public, or on private banking. We simply ask that the United States Government shall establish its own banks, and branch banks in sufficient number at all points, as will enable the people to find safe deposit for their money. This will restore confidence and bring a sufficiency of money into the banks with which to do business. We ask that the people who own this money shall have fair interest on their deposits, and we ask that the people of the Nation shall have the profits that result from the handling of that money, so that we may carry forward great necessary internal improvements and give the idle multitude employment.

"We have only the kindest feeling toward bankers, capitalists and capital. We would give all the most ample opportunity to legitimately make money. We seek only to establish a system of finance whereby, through even circulation of money, all may have employment and a fair chance to accumulate profits. In this lies the future stability and prosperity of our country."

"How would you inaugurate this system of banking?"

"By educating the people. Do you believe this is right? If so go forth as an apostle. This is something that concerns you. Write it, talk it, lecture upon it. Require of your congressmen that they endorse it and work for it.

"There may be no direct profit in it to you, just now, but there will be by and by. You are a part of the people in this great world. It is for your interest and our interest that they should all prosper. May we be wise enough to so do as to aid every fellow-being on earth, who may earnestly and honestly strive for the same, to obtain his fair share of the reasonable comforts of life."

A Glossary of Financial Terms,

TOGETHER WITH

New Explanations and Important Facts Relating to Money.

The following words, terms and phrases, used by bankers and writers on monetary matters, accompanied by explanations and definitions, are herewith given in order that our readers may the more easily understand the usually mysterious and unknown subject of finance.

Accepted. This is a term used when the person, upon whom a draft is drawn, agrees to pay it, by writing across the face of the draft, "Accepted, June 12, 1893, D. H. Smith."

Alloy. A metal of inferior worth mixed with a superior. Used in coin for the purpose of making a harder metal in order to resist abrasion. Our well known coins are alloyed as follows:

The alloy of gold is silver and copper. That of silver is copper.

Nickel coins contain 75 parts of copper and 25 parts of nickel. As a commodity one pound of this mixture is worth 70 cents, From one pound can be made 100 nickels, worth $5.00.

Copper coin is alloyed with tin and zinc, and as a commodity is worth 20 cents per pound. From one pound are made 160 coins worth $1.60. Copper coins are a legal tender up to 25 cents.

Assay. Examination of ore to ascertain the amount and value of metal contained therein.

Bank. The name derived from *banco*, a bench erected in the market-place for the exchange of money. First in Europe, in Italy, in 808, by the Lombard Jews, of whom some settled in Lombard Street, London, where many banks still exist.

Banks, National. See National Banks.

Banks, Private. Institutions conducted by private individuals who are responsible to no one but the depositors for the management of their banks. Through fortunate connections and favorable acquaintance these banks often do a large general banking business and are successfully conducted.

Banks, State. These institutions frequently have a savings department and are more or less under the inspection and supervision of the state. The laws regulating these banking institutions vary in different states. The state banks in Illinois are examined once a year by the auditor of the state and are required to report their condition once every three months. State and private banks in Illinois may loan money on real estate, but national banks are forbidden by law to do so.

Bank of England. Was projected by William Paterson, a Scotch merchant, to meet the difficulty experienced by William III in raising money to carry forward the war against France. In consideration of being allowed to incorporate this bank, 40 merchants, through the influence of Paterson and others, subscribed 500,000 pounds towards 1,200,000 pounds to be loaned to the government at 8 per cent. The government had heretofore been paying 20 per cent. Is largely under the supervision of the government and assists the government, though conducted for private gain.

Bank Examiner. An officer whose business it is to visit national banks from time to time, and investigate their condition as to probable solvency. The duty of the examiner is to so investigate a bank's affairs that it shall not fail. In 1892 there were 42 national bank examiners. While these examiners are ostensibly employed by the government their services are paid for by the banks.

Bank Failures. There were 154 national bank failures and 560 state and private bank failures, in the United States, during the first eight months of 1893, making in all 714. Of these 72 national banks failed in the month of July and 31 in the first week of July. Following close upon these failures, over 800 manufacturing establishments, at 210 different points, were closed, throwing 463,000 workmen out of employment. During the eight months 70 national banks and 72 state and private banks resumed.

Banking. The business of receiving the money of the people on deposit, the lending of these deposits, the issuing of bank-notes, the purchase and sale of bonds, the issuing of letters of credit, drafts, bills of exchange, etc.

Bi-Metallism. A system of having two standard metallic currencies in a country; for example, gold and silver.

Bill of Exchange. An order addressed to some person at a distance, directing him to pay a certain amount to the person in whose favor the bill is drawn or to his order.

Bullion. Consists of gold dust, gold and silver bars, nuggets, rings, pins and pieces of gold and silver of any kind not in coin.

Causes of Bank Failures. The United States comptroller of the currency reports as follows, concerning causes which bankrupted national banks, and the amount recovered by depositors in those institutions up to time of his report, in the latter part of 1892:

Maverick National, Boston. "Excessive loans to certain of its directors for speculative purposes were the cause of its failure."

Corry National, Corry, Pa. "False debits to other banks, criminal violations of law." Depositors had recovered 50 per cent at time of report.

California National, San Diego, Cal. "Schemes and deals in the interest of the officers of the bank and the local community" 30 per cent paid to depositors at time of report.

Cheyenne National, Cheyenne, Wyo. "Cashier and president misappropriated an amount equal to the entire capital of the bank. Management reckless and extravagant." Depositors recovered 25 per cent.

First National, Wilmington, N. C. "Failure due to speculation and robbery by the cashier. False entries on the books to deceive the examiner."

Depositors recovered 30 per cent.

First National, Downs, Kan. "Management was extravagant and the cashier was reckless." Depositors recovered 25 per cent.

Bell County National, Temple, Texas, "False entries in the books made to conceal misappropriations and forgery." Depositors recovered 30 per cent.

First National, Silver City, N. Mex.

"Fraudulent entries were made on the books. Charges of embezzlement, placed in the hands of the United States Attorney." 20 per cent paid to depositors.

Vincennes National, Vincennes, Ind. "Bank was connected with firms engaged in grain speculations. Correspondence found which connected the president with heavy losses." Depositors received 30 per cent.

Certified Check. This is a regular check which ,after being filled has been taken to the bank, where the bank official has certified on it that the amount specified is in the bank and will be paid when the check is presented.

Certificate of Deposit. A paper signed by an official in the bank, certifying that the amount specified, on the paper, has been deposited in the bank.

Checkbook. This is a book of blank orders, or checks as they are called, with a margin on which to make a memorandum of date, amount, and to whom the check is given. When the check is filled and paid out, it goes to the bank where the individual deposits money while the memorandum remains in the book.

Clearing House. A place in any large city where a representative from each bank meets the other representatives from banks, at a certain hour in the day. At that meeting each bank is credited with the total demands it holds against all other banks, and is debited with the total demands which the other banks hold against it and either pays or receives the balance in money.

Clearing House Certificates. The clearing house association, in times of financial stringency, may permit banks belonging to its organization to pay their indebtedness to the clearing house in clearing house certificates. These are issued to a bank, having payments to make, to the extent of 75 per cent on the market value of any railroad or other marketable stocks, notes or bonds which they may deposit. These certificates take the place of currency, draw six per cent interest and pass among banks in settlement of all balances.

Coining. The act of stamping and converting metals into coins to be used as money.

Coins. In 1837 the U. S. Congress enacted a mint law by which the French standard of fineness of 900-1,000, for both gold and silver, was adopted. The weight of the silver dollar to be 412½ grains and the lesser silver coins to be in proportion. See the following:

1849. Then were added to the coinage, the gold double eagle, worth $20 and the gold dollar containing 25.8 grains, the latter to be the unit of value.

1853. The weight of the half dollar was reduced from 206¼ grains to 192 grains and smaller coins in proportion, to prevent the coins being exported to foreign countries, where they were sold for bullion, bullion at that time being worth more than coin.

1864. The bronze cent was introduced, consisting of 95 per cent of copper, and 5 per cent of tin and zinc; weight 48 grains. Also a two-cent copper piece weighing 96 grains.

1865. A three-cent coin was made in this year which was three-fourths copper and one-fourth nickel, weighing 30 grains.

1866. A five-cent piece was coined, being three-fourths copper and one-fourth nickel, weighing 77.16 grains.

1873. The fineness of gold and silver to be nine-tenths pure. The alloy of silver coin to consist of copper. The alloys of gold coins to be copper, or copper and silver; the silver in no case to exceed one-tenth of the whole alloy. The rates determined upon then, prevail at the present time. The gold coins, are a one dollar (no longer coined) of 25.8 grains. A quarter eagle ($2.50) containing 64.5 grains, a three-dollar piece, 77.4 grains, (no longer coined) a half eagle, ($5) having 129 grains;

an eagle, ($10) having 258 grains, and a double eagle, ($20) containing 516 grains. These are legal tender to any amount.

The silver coins are a "trade dollar" weighing 420 grains; intended for the convenience of commerce with China and Japan; the standard dollar of 412½ grains, a half-dollar, or fifty-cent piece, containing 192.9 grains; a quarter dollar and a dime, containing respectively one-half and one-fifth the weight of the half dollar. Except the trade dollar, these silver coins, after 1873, to be a legal tender at their nominal value for any amount, not exceeding five dollars on any one payment.

The yet smaller coins to be a five-cent and a three-cent piece, three-fourths copper, and one-fourth nickel, weighing respectively 77.16 and 30 grains, and a one-cent piece of 95 per cent copper and 5 per cent tin and zinc, weighing 48 grains, which are a legal tender, at their nominal value, for any amount, not exceeding 25 cents, in any one payment.

Coins of Foreign Nations. The standard metal money of foreign nations and the unit coin by which they measure values, as the people of the United States measure values by the dollar, is given in the following:

Argentine Republic. Use both gold and silver coin. The silver "peso," worth 96½ cents, is the standard monetary unit of the country.

Austria-Hungary. Gold, the standard metal of the country. The "florin," worth 34 cents, the monetary unit.

Belgium, gold and silver. The "franc," worth 19.3 cents, is the monetary unit. The silver 5 franc piece is the dollar of the country.

Bolivia uses silver, the "boliviano," worth 69 cents, being the monetary unit.

Brazil has a gold standard, but the silver "milreis," worth 54½ cents, is the monetary unit.

British North America has a gold standard; the "dollar," is the monetary unit.

Central America adopts silver. The monetary unit is the "peso," worth 69 cents.

Chili, gold and silver; "peso," worth 91.2 cents, the monetary unit.

China, silver; the "tael," worth about $1.02, the monetary unit.

Cuba, gold and silver; the "peso," worth 92.6 cents, the monetary unit.

Denmark, gold; the silver "crown," worth 27 cents, the unit.

Egypt, gold; the "pound," worth about $4.94, is their unit. The silver coins are the "piastres," of various denominations, from 5 cents up.

France, gold and silver; the "franc," worth 19.3 cents, the unit.

German Empire, gold; the "mark," worth about 24 cents, the unit.

Great Britian, gold; the "pound," worth about $4.86½ cents, the unit.

Greece, gold and silver; the "drachma," worth 19⅕ cents, the unit.

Hayti, gold and silver; the "gourde," worth 96½ cents, the unit.

India, gold and silver; the "rupee," worth 32½ cents, the unit.

Italy, gold and silver; the "lira," worth 19⅓ cents, the unit.

Japan, gold and silver; the "yen," worth 74½ cents, the unit.

Liberia, gold; the "dollar," worth 100 cents, the unit.

Mexico, silver; the "dollar," worth 75 cents, the unit.

Netherlands, gold and silver; the "florin," worth 40 cents, the unit.

Norway, gold; the "crown," worth 26⅔ cents, the unit

Peru, silver; the "sol," worth 69 cents, the unit.

Portugal, gold; the "milreas," worth $1.08, the unit.

Russia, silver; the "rouble," worth 55⅓ cents, the unit.

Spain, gold and silver: the "peseta," worth 19⅓ cents, the unit.

Sweden, gold; the "crown," worth 26⅔ cents, the unit.

Switzerland, gold and silver; the "franc," worth 19⅓ cents, the unit.

Turkey, gold; the "piastre," worth 4½ cents, the unit.

United States, gold; the "dollar," worth 100 cents, the unit.

Venezuela, silver; the "bolivar," worth 13⅗ cents, the unit.

Collateral Security. Security that is given along with the promisory note of the borrower, to insure payment.

Consols. Bonds, issued by the English government. These usually bear 3 per cent interest, per annum. Also issued by the United States in 1865-67.

Copper. Is said to have been first discovered in Cyprus, spoken of in the Bible (Ezra VIII. 27) 457 B. C. Was used by the early Romans, in rude form, as money. Was first coined in England in 1665, and came largely into use in 1689, but had been coined in Ireland, as early as 1339, and in Scotland in 1406.

Currency. That which is received and paid out as a representative of value is usually designated as currency. Money which will not pass current, such as foreign coins, trade dollars etc., would not be considered currency.

Currency Certificates. Certificates of deposit issued at the United States treasury and sub-treasuries of the United States, to national banks on their deposits of United States notes. When banks become overloaded with this kind of paper money they deposit the same at the sub-treasury and receive these certificates, which are in denomination of $5,000 and $10,000. They have little circulation except among bankers.

Debenture Bonds. Are promissory notes, or bonds, given for money borrowed, the payment of which is ensured by lein on first moneys received. Thus the bonds given for money borrowed to maintain an exposition, the security being the money received at the gates, might be termed debenture bonds.

Demonetizing. The act of changing a value by restricting the coinage, use and circulation of a certain metal. Thus silver bullion, in consequence of limiting the coinage of silver, is a commodity, which, in amount necessary to make $1, in 1893, is worth 56 cents. When coined, this amount of bullion becomes worth, in coin, $1. Before demonetization, by Act of Congress, in 1873, the bullion was worth as much or more than coin. After demonetization, the bullion, in value declined. Before demonetization, if an individual had $100 in silver, in one pile, and $100, in gold, in another pile, and a fire had occurred, the metal, though melted and run together, in each case, if taken to the mint, would have yielded the owner $100. After demonetization the mass of melted gold would yield $100, but the pile of melted silver would sell, in 1893, for only $56.

Drafts. This document is similar to a Bill of Exchange, and Letter of Credit in its purpose. Thus a bank in Chicago will deposit a certain amount of money in a bank in New York. A customer of the Chicago bank, wishing to pay a sum of money to any person in the East will buy a draft of the Chicago bank for the amount to be paid, the draft so purchased being sent by mail, to the person to whom money is due.

Duties on Imports. Charges fixed by law on goods coming into the country from foreign lands.

Eagle. An ancient coin of Ireland, about 1272. So named from the figure impressed upon it. The American gold coinage of Eagles, worth each $10, was begun Dec. 6, 1792.

Exchange. In finance is sometimes an abbreviation from Bill of Exchange, but usually has reference to the expense of transmitting certain amounts of money to different parts of the country, or to foreign countries.

Farthing. A copper coin, one-fourth the value of a penny. First coined in England, in 1665. Half-farthing, first coined in 1843.

Fiat. In monetary matters it is the giving by authority of law, money value to that which, without government decree, would have less value or no value.

Financial History of the United States Since 1837. Record of dates, when, through Acts of Congress, bonds, notes and certificates have been issued and loans made on which interest has been paid. The amounts here mentioned were sometimes authorized to be issued for the purpose of changing Government bonds into those bearing a lower rate of interest; consequently these figures do not always mean an increase of the public debt. While Congress, frequently in these loans, authorized a larger amount than is here specified, these are the amounts actually issued and paid out.

Oct. 12, 1837, May 21, 1838, March 2, 1839, March 31, 1840, Feb. 15, 1841, Jan. 31, 1842, Aug 31, 1842, March 3, 1843, issued "Treasury Notes Prior to 1846" for $47,002,900, running one and two years, at 6 per cent interest.

1846 July 22. "Treasury Notes for 1846," $7,687,800, to run 1 year, 1-10 to 5 2-5 per cent interest.

1846 Aug. 10, "Mexican Indemnity;" bonds for $303,573,92, running 5 years, at 5 per cent interest.

1847 Jan. 28, "Treasury Notes of 1847," for $26,122,100, running 1 and 2 years, at 5 2-5 and 6 per cent.

1847 Jan. 28, "Loan of 1847," for $28,230,350, running 20 years, at 6 per cent interest.

1847 Feb. 11, "Bounty Land Scrip,"
for $233,075. Indefinite time, at 6 per cent interest

1850 Sept. 9, "Texan Indemnity Stock," for $5,000,000, running 14 years, at 5 per cent.

1857 Dec. 23, "Treasury Notes of 1857," for $52,778,900, for 1 year.
Interest from 3 to 6 per cent.

1858 June 14, "Loan of 1858," for $20,000,000, to run 15 years, at 5 per cent interest.

1860 June 22, "Loan of 1860," for $7,022,000, to run 10 years, at 5 per cent interest.

1861 Feb. 8, "Loan of February 1861, (1881)" for $18,415,000, to run 10 or 20 years, at 6 per cent interest.

1861 Mar. 2, "Treasury Notes of 1861," for $35,364,450, to run 60 days or 2 years, at 6 per cent interest.

1861 March 2, "Oregon War Debt," $1,090, 850 to run 20 years, at 6 per cent interest.

1861 July 17. "Loan of July and August 1861, (1881)" $50,000,000 to run 20 years, at 7 per cent interest.

1861 Aug. 5, "Loan" $139,321,350 to extend 20 years at 6 per cent interest.

1861 July 17, Aug. 5, 1861, Feb. 12, 1862, "Old Demand Notes," $60,030,000 to run indefinitely. No interest.

1861 July 17, "Seven-Thirties of 1861," $139,999,750 to extend 3 years at 7 and 3-10 per cent interest.

1862 Feb. 25, March 3. 1864, Jan. 28, 1865, "Five-Twenties of 1862," for $514,771,600 to run 5 or 20 years at 6 per cent interest.

1862 Feb. 25, "Legal Tender Notes," for $150,000,000 to run indefinitely. Exchangeable for U. S. 6 per cent bonds.

1862 July 11, "Legal Tender Notes," for $150,000,000, to run indefinitely. Exchangeable for 6 per cent bonds.

1862 Feb. 25, Mar. 17, 1862, July 11, 1862, June 30, 1864. "Temporary Loan," for $716,049,247, to run indefinitely at 4, 5, and 6 per cent interest.

1862 Mar. 1. May 17, 1662, Mar. 3, 1863, "Certificates of Indebtedness," for $561,753,241.65, to run 1 year, at 6 per cent interest.

1862 July 17, Mar. 3, 1863, June 30, 1864, "Fractional Currency," for $368,720,079, for indefinite time at no interest.

1863 March 3, "Legal Tender Notes," for $150,000,000, to run indefinitely. Exchangeable for 6 per cent bonds.

1863 Mar. 3, "Loan of 1863," for $75,000,000, to run 17 years, at 6 per cent interest.

1863 Mar. 3, "One Year Notes of 1863," for $44,520,000, to run 1 year, at 5 per cent interest.

1863 Mar. 3, "Two Year Notes of 1863," for $166,480,000, to run 2 years, at 5 per cent interest.

1863 Mar. 3, "Gold Certificates," $5,782,920 outstanding in 1882, running indefinitely. No interest.

1863 Mar. 3. "Compound Interest Notes," for $266,595,440, to run 3 years, at 6 per cent, compound.

1864 Mar. 3, "Ten Forties of 1864," for $196,118,300, to run 10 or 40 years at 5 per cent interest.

1864 June 30, "Five Twenties of June, 1864," for $125,561,300, running 5 or 20 years at 6 per cent interest.

1864 June 30, Jan. 28, 1865, Mar. 3, 1865, "Seven Thirties of 1864 and 1865," for $829,992,500, running 3 years, at 7 and 3-10 per cent.

1864 July 1, "Navy Pension Fund," for $14,000,000, to run indefinitely, at 3 per cent interest.

1865 Mar. 3, April 12, 1866, "Five Twenties of 1865," for $85,155,000, to run indefinitely, at 6 per cent.

1865 Mar. 3, April 2, 1866, "Consols of 1865," for $332,998,950, to run 5 or 20 years, at 6 per cent interest.

1865 Mar. 3, April 12, 1866, "Consols of 1867," for $379,618,400, to run 5 or 20 years, at 6 per cent.

1865 Mar. 3, April 12, 1866, "Consols of 1868," for $42,539,350, for 5 or 20 years, at 6 per cent interest.

1867 Mar. 2, July 25, 1868, "Three Per Cent Certificates," for $85,155,000, to run indefinitely, at 3 per cent.

1870 July 14, "Four Per Cent Loan of 1907," for the purpose of refunding 5-20 bonds, Issued $708,980,800, in bonds to run 30 years, at 4 per cent

1870 July 14, "Four and a Half Per Cent Loan of 1891," for the purpose of refunding the 5-20 bonds. Issued $185,000,000, to run 15 years, at 4½ per cent interest.

1870 July 14, "Five Per Cent Loan of 1881," to be used in refunding the 5-20 bonds $486,043,000, to run 10 years, at 5 per cent interest.

1873 Dec. 17, "Five Per Cent Loan of 1881," $13,957,000, for the purpose of exchanging bonds.

1875 Jan. 14, "Five Per Cent Loan of 1881," for silver to redeem fractional currency, for $17,494,150, to run 10 years, at 5 per cent interest.

1875 Mar. 3, "Five Per Cent Loan of 1881," (to pay J. B. Eads) for building Jetties, $500,000, to run 10 years, at 5 per cent interest.

1875 Jan. 14, "Four and a Half Per Cent Loan of 1891," for purposes of resumption. Issued $65,000,000, to run 15 years, at 4½ per cent.

1875 Jan. 14, "Four Per Cent Loan," $30,500,000, for 30 years, at 4 per cent; June 9, 1872, "Certificate of Deposit," $64,780,000, at par; Feb. 28, 1878, "Silver Certificates," $51,166,530, at par; Feb. 26, 1879, "Refunding Certificates," $40,012,750, the latter to run indefinitely at 4 per cent, interest.

Financial Legislation. The following are the principal acts by the United States Congress, relating to gold and silver coinage in the past one hundred years:

1785 Adopted the Spanish silver dollar as the unit of our money, making it the lawful dollar and standard.

1792 Ratio between silver and gold fixed at 15 to 1; meaning that every fifteen pounds weight of pure silver should be equal in value, in all payments, with one pound of pure gold, and so in proportion as to any greater or less quantities of the respective metals.

Free coinage was established, which permitted the owner of gold or silver bullion to bring the same to the mint, have the same assayed and converted into coin, the owner receiving coin of the same weight as the bullion brought to the mint.

The standard dollar made to contain 371¼ grains of pure silver and 416 grains of standard silver. All gold and silver coins struck and issued from the mint were made a lawful tender for all debts; and those of less than full weight at values proportional to their respective weights.

The dollars of Mexico, Peru, Chili and Central America, weighing not less than 415 grains each, were made legal value and to pass current as lawful money; and also the five-franc piece of France, weighing not less than 384 grains, to pass current at 93 cents.

1834 Weight of ten-dollar gold coins reduced from 247½ grains to 232 grains, pure gold, which, in comparison with the pure silver in the dollar, made the ratio 16 to 1, instead of 15 to 1.

1837 By reducing the alloy in the coin the weight of the silver dollar was reduced to 412½ grains, and fractional silver in the same proportion; the legal tender privilege to continue on the dollar and smaller silver coins.

1854 To prevent the fractional silver coins from being exported to Europe where the ratio was 15½ to 1, the silver half-dollar was reduced, in 1834, from 206¼ grains to 192 grains. Because of this less weight in the smaller silver coins, their legal tender character, in 1854, was reduced to $5; the standard silver dollar remaining a lawful legal tender, in the payment of all debts, up to 1873.

1873 The law made to read "That the gold coins. of the United States shall be a one-dollar piece, which, at the standard weight of twenty-five and eight-tenths grains, shall be the unit of value," etc. Provision made for all the gold coins, for the fractional silver coins, and for a trade dollar of 420 grains. The trade dollar and silver coins made a legal tender to the amount of $5, and gold coins to be a legal tender in payment of all debts whatsoever. The coinage was not stopped by direct language, but the legal tender character of silver being limited in payment to $5, indicated preference for gold.

1876 The trade dollar withdrawn as a legal tender in any amount, and its coinage to cease except when required for export. Thenceforth silver bullion and trade dollars became a commodity.

1878 An effort made to restore free coinage by the Bland Act, which permitted the purchase of silver bullion at its market value, to be coined into silver dollars, at the rate of not less than $2,000,000 nor more than $4,000,000 per month. Made a legal tender for all debts, public and private, except when otherwise expressly stipulated in the contract.

Free coinage not permitted, as the law only allowed for the purchase of bullion at its market value and the storage of silver dollars until called for. Was not made fully a legal tender, as the contract might provide otherwise.

1890 The Sherman law provided for the purchase of 4,500,000 ounces of silver monthly, against which silver certificates were issued. The law of 1878, known as the Bland Act, repealed.

By the law of 1873, free coinage of silver ceased, in the United States, and the government began storing silver in the treasury vaults, silver certificates taking its place in circulation. See "Free Coinage."

Finances of the United States. On August 31, 1893, the debt of the United States was $1,526,575,139.63. At that time there were in the United States treasury, $565,614,881.00, making the debt, after deducting the cash in the treasury, $960.960,258.63.

Statement of general stock of money coined and issued, Sept. 1, 1893.

Kinds of Money.	General Stock, Coined or Issued.	In Treasury.
Gold Coin	$ 547,516,035	$ 78,049,667
Standard Silver Dollars	419,332,450	357,677,820
Subsidiary Silver	77,036,067	12,700,829
Gold Certificates	80,979,419	565,370
Silver Certificates	329,088,504	2,882,168
Treasury Notes, Act of July 14, 1890	149,881,958	4,461,749
United States Notes	346,681,016	15,042,958
Currency Certificates	5,665,000	60,000
National Bank Notes	$ 198,980,368	$ 3,157,587
Totals	$ 2,155,160,817	$ 474,598,146

Kinds of Money.	Amount in Circulation, * September 1, 1893.	Amount in Circulation, Sept. 1, 1892.
Gold Coin	$ 469,466,368	$ 411,154,411
Standard Silver Dollars	61,654,630	57,622,886
Subsidiary Silver	64,335,238	63,897,139
Gold Certificates	80,414,049	128,387,379
Silver Certificates	326,206,336	328,289,145
Treasury Notes, Act of July 14, 1890	145,420,209	104,114,086
United States Notes	331,638,060	317,548,420
Currency Certificates	5,605,000	22,210,000
National Bank Notes	195,822,781	166,033,118
Totals	$ 1,680,562,671	$ 1,509,256,584

* In consequence of lack of confidence in banks, and money being hidden, but a small proportion of this money is in active circulation.
The population of the United States September 1. 1893, was estimated at 67,186,-000; according to which the circulation, per capita, should be $ 25.01.

Fiscal Year. The period of twelve months, during which time a record is kept of the revenues and expenditures of the government, at the end of which (June 30,) a report is made by the United States treasurer.

Five-twenty Bonds. These are government bonds which may be paid in five years, or the time in which they may be paid may be extended to twenty years. Ten-forty bonds, mean payment between ten, and forty years.

Fractional Currency. A paper issued during and after the war, in denominations of 5, 10, 25 and 50 cents. Because of its convenience, when sending small sums by mail, it was usually known as "postal currency."

Free Coinage of Silver. Means that the mints of the United States shall be open to coin into money, free of charge, all the silver that shall be brought to the mint by individuals or corporations. That the coins so made from the bullion brought to the mint, pound for pound, instead of being stored in the government vault, shall be allowed to be taken from the mint and put into circulation by the individuals who furnish the silver. The advocates of free coinage claim that there are to-day on earth no more than sixteen pounds of silver to one pound of gold; that many silver mines are worked out, that gold mines are being opened as rapidly as silver mines, and therefore, while there should be free coinage for individuals, as there was before 1873, the ratio should still continue at 16 to 1.

Funding the Five-twenties into the Ten-forties. Means selling bonds which run ten or forty years, and with the money thus borrowed, usually at a lower rate of interest, paying off the five-twenty bonds.

Gold. Formerly found most abundantly in Africa, Japan, and South America. Discovered in the latter country in 1492, by the Spaniards, in California in 1847, in Australia in 1851, in New Zealand in 1861, in South Africa in 1868.

Gold Certificates. Paper-notes issued by the government in denominations of not less than twenty dollars, on deposits of gold bullion. These certificates circulate as paper money, and will be redeemed in gold coin when presented to the United States treasury. They are also received in payment for duties on imports and in payment of interest on the public debt. They are in denominations of 20, 50, 100, 500, 1,000, 5,000, and 10,000 dollars.

Gold and Silver, Total Production. The following is the estimated total production of gold and silver in the several countries:

GOLD FROM ALL COUNTRIES.

SILVER FROM ALL COUNTRIES.

Estimated total yield of gold in all countries, from 1493 to recent date.	Estimated total yield of silver in all countries, from 1493 to recent date.
United States.............$ 905,126,015	Mexico...................$2,600,290,857
Australasia....................889,063,800	Bolivia.....................1,289,990,040
New Granada...............506,501,675	Peru.......................1,065,357,084
Brazil.........................509,347,107	Austria-Hungary............264,961,603
Russia.........................507,749,653	Other European Countries...251,988,604
Africa.........................359,325,340	United States...............179,874,123
Austria-Hungary............226,248,247	Chili........................89,024,208
Bolivia........................144,308,100	Russia.......................82,880,591
Mexico........................130,174,306	Various Countries...........64,244,000
Chili..........................129,467,140	Germany.....................260,731,339
Various Countries............74,458,340	
Peru...........................80,327,582	Total............... $ 6,159,241,948
$ 4,643,087,395	

Gold Nuggets. The Sarah Sands nugget, found at Ballarat, Australia, weighed 130 pounds troy, and was worth $31,200. The Blanche Barkly nugget, dug up at Kingower, Australia, weighed 145 pounds, and was worth $34,800. The largest ever found was the Welcome nugget, found at Ballarat. It weighed 184 pounds and sold for $50,000.

Gold and Silver Production. The amount of gold and silver produced in the United States, and in the several states, is given in the following tables:

WHERE GOLD COMES FROM.		WHERE SILVER COMES FROM.	
Deposit of domestic productions of gold at the U. S. Mints from 1793 to June 30, 1889.		Deposit of domestic productions of silver at the U. S. Mints from 1793 to June 30, 1889.	
State.	*Amount.*	*State.*	*Amount.*
California......... .....$ 751,894,978 47		Nevada................. $ 95,679,597 22	
Montana................ .....64,207,386 18		Colorado.................24,400,670 27	
Colorado.................. 56,120,058 09		Utah.......................19,124,512 78	
Dakota...............33,531,413 61		Montana..............15,068,146 87	
Idaho......................30,989,827 50		Arizona...................13,782,727 53	
Nevada..................26,498,421 85		New Mexico...............6,451,072 71	
Oregon..............19,996,536 67		California....4,043,312 24	
North Carolina............11,470,874 81		Michigan....................3,773,272 75	
Georgia....................8,738,252 40		Idaho......................1,744,926 43	
Arizona................4,765,641 69		Dakota.....................841,195 75	
New Mexico............ ..3,725,991 36		Oregon.....................73,376 53	
Virginia...............1,737,470 41		North Carolina........... ...55,699 13	
South Carolina.........1,727,423 50		Wyoming.................12,640 91	
Utah.....................986,310 81		Alaska 5,727 41	
Wyoming...............787,380 22		Texas 5,187 18	
Alaska......................564,036 41		Washington.................3,189 38	
Washington...............538,044 48		Pennsylvania...............2,588 47	
Alabama..................233,773 38		South Carolina 2,008 49	
Michigan.................133,700 03		Massachusetts...............,917 56	
Tennessee........ ....89,262 93		Georgia.......................859 85	
Vermont.....................85,598 21		Virginia.........................355 53	
New Hampshire............ ...11,283 79		Alabama......................128 54	
Maryland................ ....7,221 37		Vermont.........................49 94	
Maine........................5,638 20		Nebraska......................22 84	
Texas.....................3,418 67		Maine..........................22 00	
Nebraska................ 2,078 76		Tennessee.....................11 66	
Pennsylvania..............1,138 34		Maryland.......................4 26	
Indiana..............................40 13		New Hampshire.....................87	
Other Sources..... ....38,979,747 53		Other Sources...........42,408,554 77	
	$ 1,057,922,887 96		$ 227,494,790 78
Refined bullion,........ $ 288,183,599 25		Refined bullion.... ..... $ 271,833,633 29	

TOTAL GOLD AND SILVER From 1493 to recent date.		TOTAL OF PRECIOUS METALS From earliest times.
Mexico.................. $ 2,730,455,055		The total production of precious metals from surface and mines of the earth, from the earliest period to the close of 1879, is estimated to be as follows:
Bolivia....................1,431,368,047		
United States............1,175,000,138		
Peru.................. ...1,145,684,666		
Australia....................889,963,800		Gold................ ....$14,068,375,000
New Granada........ 596,501,675		Silver....................11,315,000,000
Russia........ .. ..590 ,629,944		
Brazil........ ....509, 347,107		Total..............$ 25,383,375,000
Austria-Hungary..... 491,209,850		
Africa.................359,325,340		A cubic foot of pure gold weighs 1,203 pounds and 10 ounces.
Germany...................269,731,229		A cubic foot of pure silver weighs 625 pounds and 13 ounces.
Other European countries..251,888,604		
Chili....................218,491,428		A ton of pure gold is worth $ 602,799.21.
Various countries.........142,702,343		A ton of silver coin is worth $ 37,704.84.
Total........... $ 10,802,329,3430		

$ 1,000,000 gold coin weigh 3,865 8 pounds avoirdupois.
$ 1,000,000 silver coin weigh 58,929.9 pounds avoirdupois.

Government Receipts and Expenditures. That our readers may know our sources of income, why and for what moneys are expended, during the year, and the amounts, we herewith give the condensed report of the United States treasurer for the fiscal year 1892. The expense of salaries for congressmen and salaries in all the various departments are included under the head of "civil establishment."

The revenues of the government from all sources for the fiscal year ending June 30, 1892, were:

From customs	$177,452,964 15
From internal revenue	153,971,072 57
From profits on coinage, bullion deposits and assays	2,020,512 39
From sales of public lands	3,261,875 58
From fees—consular, letters patent, and land	3,130,437 06
From sinking-fund for Pacific railway	1,828,771 46
From tax on national banks	1,261,338 11
From customs fees, fines, penalties, and forfeitures	900,249 66
From repayment of interest by Pacific railways	962,437 67
From sales of Indian lands	817,813 23
From Soldiers' Home, permanent fund	194,385 45
From tax on seal-skins	46,749 23
From immigrant fund	330,128 65
From sales of Government property	236,498 38
From deposits for surveying public lands	149,906 21
From sales of ordnance material	101,242 35
From sales of condemned naval vessels	31,854 12
From sale of old custom-house, Milwaukee, Wis	64,000 00
From sale of land, Brooklyn navy-yard	593,860 33
From Smithsonian fund	200,000 00
From navy pension and navy hospital funds, etc	1,118,155 25
From depredations on public lands	61,623 85
From the District of Columbia	2,967,044 71
From proceeds District of Columbia ten-year funding bonds	2,412,744 00
From miscellaneous sources	783,059 83
From postal service	70,930,475 98
Total receipts	**$425,808,260 22**

The expenditures for the same period were:

For the civil establishment, including foreign intercourse, public buildings, collecting the revenues, deficiency in postal revenues, rebate of tax on tobacco, refund of direct taxes, French spoilation claims, District of Columbia, and other miscellaneous expenses	$99,841,988 61
For the military establishment, including rivers and harbors, forts, arsenals, and seaport defenses	46,895,456 30
For the naval establishment, including construction of new vessels, machinery, armament, equipment, and improvement at navy-yards	29,174,138 08
For Indian service	11,150,577 67
For pensions	134,583,052 79
For interest on the public debt	23,378,116 23
For postal service	70,930,475 98
Total expenditures	**$415,953,806 56**
Leaving a surplus of	**$8,914,453 66**

Government Bonds. An obligation entered into by the government in which it agrees to pay a certain stipulated sum at a stated time. Is similar to a promissory note. When the government wants to borrow money it prepares a bond or bonds, handsomely engraved, with coupon attached, indicating the amount of interest, and when it will pay the interest, usually every six months. These bonds are given to certain parties, usually bankers, to sell to any one who will buy and pay for them. It is thus that the government borrows money from any one who is willing to take these government notes. During the war of the rebellion the United States government sold their bonds, bearing 6 per cent interest, interest payable in gold. As gold commanded a premium, these bonds were very much in demand when first issued. The interest and principal of government bonds, which constitute the public debt, are required to be paid in coin of standard value.

Hill Banking System. This is a plan for the government owner-ship of banks, the proposition being to establish the government bank, at all central points, in sufficient number to care for all the money of the people; the postmaster in the back districts, where there are no banks, being authorized to receive the people's money and send the same to the nearest banks. In this plan the government is simply the custodian of the people's money, receives it on deposit, guards the depositor against loss, allows 3 per cent on time deposits, and loans at a uniform rate of 4 per cent. It is essentially a straight banking system as banking is done to-day. The government invests nothing in the enterprise, but guarantees the depositor against any loss from bank failures and receives a commission on loans. The result is, because of implicit confidence, the bank is always full of people's good, sound money; and borrowers, who can furnish safe security, can always obtain money at reasonable interest. Details of the system are given in "Money Found," (pages 9–94) which show that when people can safely place their money in the bank they will do so and transact their business with checks. These checks become the abundant "Money Found," with which to do business.

Ingot. A mass of gold, silver, or other metal, cast in a mold.

Interest. Compensation for the use of money loaned. Was termed usury, according to the Scriptures, 1491 B. C. Was permitted by the Jews to be taken from strangers, but not from one of their own bretheren. Was prohibited by the English parliament from 1341 until the 15th century. During that period the Jews were often prosecuted and banished as usurers because of taking interest.

Interest in Different States. The following are the prevailing rates of interest in the several states and the penalties for usury:

States and Territories.	Legal rate of Interest.	Rate allowed by Contract.	Penalties for Usury.
	per cent.	per cent.	
Alabama	8	8	Forfeiture of entire interest.
Arizona	7	Any rate.	
Arkansas	6	10	Forfeiture of principal and interest.
California	7		Any rate.
Colorado	8	Any rate.	
Connecticut	6	6	
Dakota	7	12	Forfeiture of interest.
Delaware	6	6	Forfeiture of principal.
District of Columbia	6	10	Forfeiture of entire interest.
Florida	8	10	Forfeiture of interest.

Interest in Different States. The following are the prevailing rates of interest in the several states and the penalties for usury:

States and Territories.	Legal rate of Interest.	Rate allowed by Contract.	Penalties for Usury.
	per cent.	per cent.	
Georgia	7	8	Forfeiture of excess of interest.
Idaho	10	18	Forfeiture of 10 per cent of the debt.
Illinois	5	7	Forfeiture of entire interest.
Indiana	6	8	Forfeiture of excess of interest.
Iowa	6	8	Ten per cent on entire contract.
Kansas	6	10	Forfeiture twice ex. above 10 pr. ct.
Kentucky	6	6	Forfeiture of excess of interest.
Louisiana	5	8	Forfeiture of entire interest.
Maine	6	Any rate.	
Maryland	6	6	Forfeiture of excess of interest.
Massachusetts	6	Any rate.	
Michigan	6	8	Forfeiture of excess of interest
Minnesota	7	10	Forfeiture of interest and cost.
Mississippi	6	10	Forfeiture of excess of interest.
Missouri	6	8	Forfeiture of entire interest.
Montana	10	Any rate.	
Nebraska	7	10	Forfeiture of interest and costs.
Nevada	7	Any rate.	
New Hampshire	6	6	Forfeiture of thrice the ex. and costs.
New Jersey	6	6	Forfeiture of interest and cost.
New Mexico	6	12	
New York	6	6*	Forfeiture of twice ex. of interest.
North Carolina	6	8	Forfeiture of entire interest.
Ohio	6	8	Forfeiture of excess above 6 per ct.
Ontario, Canada	6	Any rate.	
Oregon	8	10	Forfeiture of principal and interest.
Pennsylvania	6	6	Forfeiture of excess of interest.
Quebec, Can	6	Any rate.	
Rhode Island	6	Any rate.	
South Carolina	7	8	Forfeiture of entire interest.
Tennessee	6	6	Forfeiture of ex. of int. and $100 fine.
Texas	6	10	Forfeiture of all interest.
Utah	8	Any rate.	
Vermont	6	6	Forfeiture of excess of interest.
Virginia	6	8*	Forfeiture of excess of 6 per cent.
Washington	10	Any rate.	
West Virginia	6	6*	Forfeiture of excess of interest.
Wisconsin	7	10	Forfeiture of entire interest.
Wyoming	12	Any rate.	

*Except in cases defined by Statutes of the State.

Latin Union. In financial affairs this relates to the international monetary conference, held in Paris, France, in which an agreement was signed, Nov. 8, 1885, that for a certain number of years France, Italy, Belgium and Switzerland should maintain the same system of coinage. The unrestricted coinage of silver was suspended in the countries of the Latin Union in 1873.

Legal Tender. That which the law authorizes to be tendered in payment of debts.

Legal Tender Notes. A paper currency authorized by the government, which is lawful money and can be tendered in payment for any debts, public and private, except when otherwise expressly stipulated in the contract. Is issued in denominations of 1, 2, 5, 10, 20, 50, 100, 500, and 1,000 dollars.

Lawyers in Financial Legislation. During the last twenty years, up to 1891, the majority of the members, during various sessions of congress, have been lawyers, as seen in the following:

Which Congress.	During what years.	No. of Senators.	No. of Lawyers in Senate.	No. of Representatives.	No. of Lawyers in House of Representatives.
..42nd	1871–1873	75	33	263	115
..43rd	1873–1875	79	30	312	149
..44th	1875–1877	82	35	316	152
..45th	1877–1879	80	35	308	169
..46th	1879–1881	76	46	302	161
..47th	1881–1883	78	39	310	151
..48th	1883–1885	78	41	346	178
..49th	1885–1887	76	42	333	187
..50th	1887–1889	76	43	333	173
..51st	1889–1891	88	49	362	205

Letter of Credit. A document, carried by most tourists in foreign countries, which authorizes certain bankers, or other persons, to pay the bearer such sums of money, as required, up to the amount deposited by the tourist before starting.

Mint. The place where gold and silver bullion is melted into bars from which are stamped coins. There are four coinage mints in the United States, located one each at Philadelphia, San Francisco, Carson City and New Orleans.

Money for Each Person. The amount of money in circulation for each person in different countries, is given in the following table which was prepared recently by the United States Director of the mint.

Countries.	The Metal which is Standard.	Gold.	Silver.	Paper.	Money per each person.
Austria	Gold	$1.00	$2.25	$6.50	$9.75
Australia	Gold	25.00	1.75		26.75
Belgium	Gold and silver	10.66	9.02	8.85	28.53
British India	Gold		3.53	11	3.64
Canada	Gold	3.56	1.11	8.89	13.56
Central America	Silver		17	67	84
Cuba	Gold and silver	10.00	1.00	20.00	31.00
Egypt	Gold	14.29	2.14		16.43
France	Gold and silver	23.53	18.30	2.72	44.55
Germany	Gold	10.42	4.48	3.12	18.02
Great Britain	Gold	14.41	2.62	1.57	18.60
Greece	Gold and silver	91	1.82	0.36	9.00
Italy	Gold and silver	4.51	1.94	6.81	13.26
Japan	Gold and silver	2.25	1.25	1.40	4.90
Mexico	Silver	43	4.31	17	4.91
Netherlands	Gold and silver	5.55	14.44	8.89	28.88
Norway and Sweden	Gold	3.72	1.16	3.14	8.02
Portugal	Gold	8.00	2.00	1.20	11.20
Russia	Silver	1.68	53	4.42	6.63
Spain	Gold and silver	5.56	6.91	5.22	17.69
South America	Silver	1.29	71	8.57	10.56
Switzerland	Gold and silver	5.00	5.00	4.67	14.67
Turkey	Gold	1.52	1.36		2.88
United States	Gold and silver	11.06	7.33	6.78	25.17

Money. Any article which may be selected by general consent, and by law, as a representative of value in exchanging one property for another. At the present time, in the United States, money consists of paper; and coins, made of gold, silver, nickel, and copper. It is first mentioned as a medium of commerce in the 23rd chapter of Genesis, when Abraham purchased a field as a sepulcher for Sarah, 1239, B. C. First made at Arzos, 894, B. C. First coined in the United States 1652. First paper money in the United States in 1690.

Money Chronology. The following are some of the leading historical facts relating to money:

1600, B. C. The Lydians, about this period, were the first to coin money.

573, B. C. Brass money coined in Rome by Servius Tullius.

928, A. D. The English mint established. Thirty-eight mints were in operation in England in the tenth century.

1460. Voyagers from Europe returned with first gold from West Africa.

1492. Columbus found considerable gold among the natives of the islands he visited.

1522. The first silver from Mexico was sent to Europe by the Spaniards from mines that had long been previously worked by the Aztecs.

1600. Holland maintained a silver monetary standard, giving gold a nominal valuation at a ratio of 14.7 to 1, from 1600 to 1816.

1652. First Colonial coinage minted in Massachusetts.

1702. A school of Mines was established at Freiberg, Saxony.

1792. The legal ratio between gold and silver, in the United States, was made 15 to 1 by the Act of Congress, creating a mint.

1803. France adopted the double monetary standard, at a ratio of 15½ to 1. Previous to the Revolution the ratio had been 15 to 1.

1816. England adopted the gold standard, by Act of Parliament.

1829. Discovery of gold mines in Georgia and first mining excitement in the United States.

1848. January 9. Marshal discovered gold at Coloma, California.

1850. Belgium adopted the single monetary standard.

1850. Quartz mining was begun in California.

1851. Discovery of gold in New South Wales, by Hargraves.

1852. Discovery of gold, in South Australia and Tasmania.

1857. Discovery of gold, in New Zealand.

1857. The German States, including Austria, adopted a single silver standard.

1859. The Comstock lode, Nevada, discovered.

1859. Discovery of gold, in Frazer River region, British Columbia.

1859. Pike's Peak excitement.

1861. Belgium returned to a double monetary standard.

1861. Gold discovered in Nova Scotia.

1862. First important discoveries of gold in Montana.

1865. Establishment of the Latin Union, consisting of France, Italy, Switzerland and Belgium, providing for a double monetary standard, at a ratio of 15½ to 1, the agreement to hold good until 1880.

1867. First international monetary conference, convened in Paris, by the French government, at which twenty nations, comprising all the important countries of Europe and America, were represented, was held.

1869. The Sutro tunnel, to open the Comstock lode, was commenced.

1871. The German Empire adopted the gold standard, and discontinued the mintage of silver.

1876. First shipment of silver-lead ore, from Leadville, Colorado.

1877. A silver commission created by the United States Congress, which reported in March.

1882. Hydraulic mining in California prohibited.

Monetary Stringency. Scarcity of money, the result of people hiding and withdrawing it from circulation, comes from fear, at a time when banks fail, that their money will be lost if they allow it to remain in banks. May be partially overcome in a locality where business men and manufacturers will agree to pay out and use each others checks until such time as confidence is generally restored, and the money of the country comes again into general circulation.

Money in Various Countries. The following are the estimated amounts of gold, silver and paper money, possessed by the different leading countries, the paper money here mentioned being not required to be redeemed in coin. The Latin Union includes several countries. (See Latin Union.)

Country.	Gold.	Silver.	Paper.
Great Britain	$550,000,000	$100,000,000*	$50,000,000
Latin Union.	975,000,000	727,000,000	250,000,000
Spain	40,000,000	158,000,000	100,000,000
Netherlands	25,000,000	65,000,000	40,000,000
German Empire	600,000,000	211,000,000	107,000,000
Austria Hungary	40,000,000	90,000,000	260,000,000
Scandinavian Union.	32,000,000	10,000,000	27,000,000
Portugal	40,000,000	10,000,000	45,000,000
Russia	250,000,000	60,000,000	500,000,000

*Subsidiary silver.

Money Order. This is issued by the government and is similar in purpose to the Bill of Exchange, Letter of Credit and Draft.

Monometallism. A system of finance in which but one metal is used as a medium of exchange and a standard of value.

National Banks, How Organized. These institutions came into existence during the war of the rebellion and were authorized by Congress, in 1864, in a law entited An Act to provide a national currency secured by a pledge of United States bonds, and to provide for the circulation and redemption thereof.

A separate bureau was provided for this department of government to be under the general control of the secretary, the chief officer of the bureau to be known as the comptroller of the currency.

That associations, for the purpose of carrying on the business of banking, may be formed of not less than five persons. In cities of more than 50,000 people, the capital of a national bank shall be not less than $200,000. That in cities of less than 50,000, and over 6,000, the capital may be $100,000, and in cities of less than 6,000, the capital may be $50,000.

That such associations may have existence for 20 years and the capital shall be divided into shares of $100 each, the stockholders to be ratably and equally liable to the extent of their stock for the debts and contracts of the bank.

That before the commencement of banking, the bank must deliver to the treasurer of the United States, government bonds, to the amount of not less than $30,000 and not less than one-third of the capital stock paid in.

That should such national bank desire to circulate notes it will be entitled to receive from the United States comptroller, 90 per cent of the par value of the bonds so deposited. Thus if there be $100,000 worth of bonds left with the treasurer, the bank shall be allowed to circulate $90,000 in national bank notes

That such national banks notes shall be received at par, in all parts of the United States, in payment for taxes, excises, public lands, and all dues to the United States, except for duties on imports. interest on the public debt, and in redemption of the national currency. The rate of interest charged shall be that which is allowed by the state where the bank is located.

No bank may have a circulation of over $500,000. That every banking association shall pay to the treasurer of the United States, in the months of January and July, one-half per cent, each half year, on the average amount of its notes in circulation, a duty of one-fourth per cent, each half year, upon the average amounts of its deposits, and a duty of one-fourth per cent, each half year, on the average amount of its capital stock beyond the amount invested in United States bonds.

Should a national bank fail, the law requires that the stockholder shall be assessed and be compelled to pay to the bank, if he can, an amount equal to the stock he held in the bank and no more. Thus if his stock was $1,000, he must pay another $1,000 to the bank to make good its loss, if the liabilities are such as to require so large an assessment.

That each of the banks in St. Louis, Louisville, Chicago, Detroit, Milwaukee, New Orleans, Cincinnati, Cleveland, Pittsburgh, Baltimore, Philadelphia, Boston, New York, Albany, Leavenworth, San Francisco and Washington, shall be required at all times to keep on hand an amount of lawful money equal to 25 per cent of the deposits, and all national banks in other cities shall keep 15 per cent.

A bank having less than the legal reserve is forbidden to increase its liabilities by making any new loans or discounts otherwise than by purchasing bills of exchange, payable at sight or to make any dividend of profits. The government may appoint a receiver to wind up the affairs of the bank if it fails to make good the reserve within thirty days after having been officially notified to do so. But three-fifths of the reserve of 15 per cent may consist of balances in banks in the reserve cities above named.

National Banks Organized Without Money. In the report of the comptroller of currency for 1892, in relation to the failure of the First National Bank at Erie, Kansas, he says: "It was developed that the stock held by the officers, had been purchased with borrowed money, the stock being pledged as collateral, and that their financial resources had always been very limited."

It is seen from the above that should five individuals, each having no money, desire to start a national bank, they can do so by borrowing money and giving their stock as security. By leading exemplary lives and taking active part in various philanthropic and useful work they may so inspire confidence as to secure the deposit of $1,000,000. After reserving 25 per cent, they may loan $750,000, at 6 per cent and receive thereon $45,000, per annum, less the office expenses and the tax on deposits. This will give each an annual income of $9,000. Should the deposits reach up to $10,000,000, which is easily probable, in a wealthy manufacturing community, the income of each of these impecunious individuals, in the beginning, may be $90,000, per year.

National Bank Notes. Bank bills issued by the several national banks. They are in denomination of 1, 2, 5, 10, 20, 50, 100, 500 and 1,000 dollars.

National Bank Failure Statement. The liabilities of banks that failed in the first eight months of 1893, according to statement of the President of the national bankers' association, which convened at Chicago, Oct 18, 1893, were over $180,000,000. Owing to lack of confidence in banks, according to statement of the U. S. Comptroller, at bankers' convention, held at Chicago, Oct. 18, 1893, the depositors drew from national banks $193,000,000, and from state and savings banks an equally large amount, within the period of three months, from May 4, to July 12, 1893.

The following were the amounts recovered from broken national banks, by depositors, up to Nov. 1, 1892, according to the report of United States comptroller of the currency:

American National Bank, Arkansas, Kan., failed Dec. 26, 1890; recovered 50 per cent.

SpringGardenNational,Philadelphia, Pa., failed May 21, 1891; recovered 20 per cent.

First National, Kansas City, Kan., failed Aug. 17, 1891; recovered 25 per cent.

First National, Ellsworth, Kan.,failed Feb. 11, 1891; recovered 30 per cent.

First National,Coldwater,Kan., failed Oct. 14, 1891; recovered 25 per cent.

Tenth National, Dallas, Tex., failed July 16, 1891; recovered 15 per cent.

Cheyenne National, Cheyenne, Wyo., failed Dec. 5, 1891; recovered 25 per cent.

First National, Red Cloud, Neb,, failed July 16, 1891; recovered 20 per cent.

Peoples National, Fayettville, N. C., failed Jan. 20, 1891; recovered 35 per cent.

First National, Meade Center, Kan., failed Dec. 24, 1890; recovered 30 per cent.

City National, Hastings, Neb., failed Jan. 14, 1891; recovered 30 per cent.

Second National, McPherson, Kan., failed Mar. 25, 1891; recovered 20 per cent.

Madison National, Madison, S. Dak., failed June 23, 1888; recovered 30 per cent.

First National, Palatka, Fla., failed Aug. 7, 1891; recovered 35 per cent.

First National, Anderson, Ind., failed Nov. 23, 1873; recovered 42 per cent.

Bell Co. National, Temple, Tex,, failed Feb. 19, 1892; recovered 30 per cent.

Keystone National, Philadelphia, Pa., failed May 9, 1891; recovered 10 per cent.

First National, Deming, N. Mex., failed Feb. 29, 1892; recovered 25 per cent.

Nickel. A white, ductile, malleable metal, ordered to be used as a substitute for bronze coinage in France in 1882.

Number of National Banks. At the close of 1892 there were 3,788 National banks in the United States, having a capital stock of $693,868,665, To secure their circulation, there were deposited in bonds $164,883,000.

Outstanding. A term applied to bonds or notes issued and not yet presented for redemption. Thus "Treasury Notes Outstanding" are treasury notes in circulation which have not yet been brought in for redemption.

Paper Money of Different Countries. The appearance of paper money of different countries may be understood from the following description:

The Bank of England note is five inches by eight in dimensions and is printed in black ink on Irish linen, water-lined paper, plaid white, with ragged edges.

The notes of the Banque de France are made of white, water-lined paper, printed in blue and black with numerous mythological and allegorical pictures, and running in denominations from the 20-franc note to the 1,000-franc.

South American currency, in most countries, is about the size and general appearance of American bills, except that cinnamon brown and slate blue are the prevailing colors and that Spanish and Portugese are the languages engraved on the face.

The German currency is printed in green and black, in denominations from 5,000 to 1,000 marks. Their later bills are printed on silk fiber paper.

The Chinese paper currency is in red, white and yellow paper, with gilt lettering and gorgeous little hand-drawn devices.

Italian notes are of all sizes, shapes and colors. The smaller bills—5 and 10 lire notes—are printed on white paper in pink, blue and carmine inks.

The 100-*ruble note of Russia* is barred from top to bottom with all the colors of the rainbow, blended as when shown through a prism. In the center, in bold relief, stands a large, finely executed vignette of the Empress Catherine I. This is in black. The other engraving is not at all intricate or elaborate but is well done in dark and light brown and black inks.

The Australian bill is printed on light-colored, thick paper, which shows none of the silk fiber marks or the geometric lines used in American currency as a protection against counterfeiting.

Paper Money of the United States, consists of five kinds, namely; "Legal tender," or United States notes, "Treasury Notes," "National Bank Notes," "Gold Certificates," and "Silver Certificates." These are each described elsewhere. They are all printed on specially prepared paper by the authorities at Washington from finely engraved plates, usually in green and black, except gold certificates which are printed in orange.

Passbook. This is a memorandum book, kept by a customer of a bank, and used by the receiving teller for the purpose of recording the amount of deposits which may be made by the customer in the bank.

Penny. The ancient silver penny was the first coin struck in England. In the beginning it was a cross, so deeply indented that it could be easly broken in two for half-pence and into four, for farthings; hence, these names. Copper penny and two-penny pieces were coined in 1797.

Pound. From the Latin *Pondus*, known in early Roman times as the Roman *Pondo*, a coin supposed to be worth about three times as much as the present British pound.

Public Debt. For the purpose of carrying forward the government in the payment of pensions, salaries of congressmen, judges and various United States officers, it is necessary to raise a revenue, in the United States, of over $400,000,000 per year. This revenue is obtained from duties on goods brought into the country from abroad, and from a tax on tobacco, spirits, oleomargerine, etc., and generally exceeds the expenditures; thus reducing the public debt.

During Jackson's administration, in 1835, the public debt was but $33,733. The war with Mexico compelled the borrowing of money and carried the debt up to over $68,000,000, in 1851, from which amount it declined to $28,600,000, in 1857. The war of the rebellion compelled more borrowing and carried the debt, on Aug. 31, 1865, up to $2,844,649,926. It is now down to about $1,500,000,000 and, with cash in the treasury, it is less than $1,000,000,000.

Public Debt of the United States. This financial statement represents the gross total public expenditure and total yearly public debt, gathered from the U. S. Treasurer's report, made July 1, of each year.

Year.	Public Expenditures.	Public Debt.	Year.	Public Expenditures.	Public Debt.
1789...	F*	....	.1845..	D .$ 30,490,408 71	$15,925,303 01
1790...	F..........	....	.1846..	D...27,632,282 90	...15,550,202 97
1791..	F.$ 3,797,436 78	$ 75,463,476 52	.1847..	D...60,520,851 74	...38,826,534 77
1792..	F.. 8,962,920 00	..77,227,924 66	.1848..	D...60,655,143 19	...47,044,862 23
1793..	F.. 6,479,977 97	..80,352,634 04	1849..	W..56,386,422 74	..63,061,858 69
1794..	F.. 9,041,593 17	. 78,427,404 77	.1850..	W..44,604,718 26	..03,452,773 55
1795..	F..10,151,240 15	. 80,747,587 39	.1851..	W..48,476,104 31	...68,304,796 02
1796..	F.. 8,367,776 84	..83,762,172 07	.1852..	W..46,712,608 83	..66,199,341 71
1797..	F.. 8,625,877 37	.82,064,479 33	.1853..	D...54,577,061 74	...59,803,117 70
1798..	F.. 8,583,618 41	.79,228,529,12	.1854..	D...75,473,170 75	..42,242,222,42
1799..	F..11,002,396 97	.78,408,669 77	.1855..	D...66,164,775 96	...35,586,956 56
1800..	F..11,952,534 12	.82,976,294 35	.1856..	D...72,726,341 57	...31,972,537 00
1801..	R..12,273,376 94	..83,038,050 80	.1857..	D...71,274,587 37	....28,699,831 85
1802..	R..13,270,487 31	.80,712,632 25	.1858...	D...82,062,186 74	....44,911,881 03
1803..	R..11,258,983 67	..77,054,686 40	.1859..	D...83,678,642 92	...58,496,837 88
1804..	R..12,615,113 72	.86,427,120 88	.1860...	D...77,055,125 65	...64,842,287 88
1805..	R..13,598,309 47	.82,312,150 50	.1861..	R...85,387,313 08	....90,580,873 72
1806..	R..15,021,196 26	..75,723,270 66	.1862..	R..565,667,563 74	.524,176,412 13
1807..	R..11,292,292 99	.69,218,398 64	.1863..	R..899,815,911 25	1,119,772,138 63
1808..	R..16,762,702 04	.65,196,317 97	.1864..	R .,295,541,114 86	1,815,784,370 57
1809..	R..13,867,226 30	..57,023,192 00	.1865..	R1,906,433,331 37	2,680,647,869 74
1810..	R..13,300,994 49	.53,173,217 52	.1866..	R1,139,344,081 95	2,773,236,173 69
1811..	R..13,592,604 86	..48,005,587 76	.1867..	R1,093,079,655 27	2,678,126,103 87
1812..	R..22,279,122 15	.45,209,737 90	.1868..	R1,069,889,970 74	2,611,687,851 19
1813..	R..39,190,520 36	..55,962,827 57	.1869..	R..584,777,996 11	2,588,452,213 94
1814..	R..38,028,230 32	.81,487,846 24	.1870..	R..702,907,842 88	2,480,672,427 81
1815..	R..39,582,493 35	.99,833,660 15	.1871..	R..691,680,858 90	2,353,211,332 32
1816..	R..48,244,495 51	127,334,933 74	.1872..	R..682,525,270 21	2,253,251,328 78
1817..	R..40,877,646 04	123,491,965 16	.1873..	R..524,044,597 91	2,234,482,993 20
1818..	R..35,104,875 40	103,466,633 83	.1874..	R..724,698,933 99	2,251,690,468 43
1819..	R..24,004,199 73	..95,529,648 28	.1875..	R .682,000,885 32	2,232,284,531 95
1820..	R..21,763,024 85	..91,015,566 15	.1876..	R..714,446,357 39	2,180,395,067 15
1821..	R..19,090,572 69	.89,987,427 66	.1877..	R..477,320,017 68	2,205,301,392 10
1822..	R..17,676,592 63	.93,546,676 98	.1878..	R..473,928,653 59	2,256,205,892 53
1823..	R..15,314,171 00	.90,875,877 28	.1879..	R..533,895,767 06	2,245,495'071 00
1824..	R..31,808,538 47	.90,269,777 77	.1880..	R..535,285,915 58	2,120,415,370 63
1825..	R..23,585,804 72	.83,788,432 71	.1881..	R..312,114,688 64	2,069,013,569 58
1826..	R..24,103,398 46	.81,054,059 99	.1882..	R..257,981,439 57	1,918,312,994 03
1827..	R..22,656,764 04	..73,987,357 20	.1883...	R..265,408,137 54	1,884,171,728 60
1828..	R..25,459,479 52	..67,475,043 87	.1884..	R..245,498,578 00	1,830,528,923 57
1829..	D..25,044,358 40	..58,421,413 67	.1885...	D..260,226,935 11	1,876,424,275 14
1830..	D..24,585,281 55	..48,565,406,50	.1886...	D..242,483,138 50	1,775,063,013 78
1831..	D..30,038,446 12	.39,123,191 68	.1887..	D..315,835,428 12	1,657,602,592 63
1832..	D..34,350,698 06	..24,332,235 18	.1888...	D..323,567,488 34	1,692,858,984 58
1833..	D..24,257,298 49	...7,001,698 83	.1889..	R..282,864,310 95	1,619,052,922 23
1834..	D..24,601,982 44	...4,760,082 08	.1890...	R..297,436,136 00	1,552,140,204 73
1835..	D..17,573,141 56	......33,733 05	.1891..	R..317,825,540 97	1,545,996,591 61
1836..	D..30,868,164 04	.....37,513 05	.1892..	R..321,645,214 35	1,588,404,144 63
1837..	D..37,265,037 15	...336,957 83	.1893..	D..341,573,424 68	1,526,575,139 63
1838..	D..39,455,438 35	..3,308,124 07	.1894..	....	....
1839..	D..37,614,936 15	.10,434,221 14	.1895..	....	....
1840..	D..28,226,533 81	..3,573,343 82	.1896.	....	....
1841..	W.31,797,530 03	...5,250,875 54	.1897..	....	....
1842..	W.32,936,876 53	.13,594,480 73	.1898..	....	....
1843..	W 12,118,105 15	.32,742,922 00	.1899...	....	....
1844..	W.33,642,010 85	.23,461,652 50	.1900...	....	...... :

* The political complexion of the different Presidential terms is indicated by a single letter opposite each year, defined as follows: *F.* Federalist; *R.* Republican; *D.* Democrat; *W.* Whig.

Quantity of Metal. The quantity of metal operated upon, in the several mints, during the fiscal year, ending June 30, 1892, exceeded 313 tons of gold, and 2,257 tons of silver.

Refunding Certificates. Consist of issue of 1879—notes of denomination not less than $10, which bear interest at four per cent per annum, and are convertible, at any time, with accrued interest, into the four per cent bonds described in the refunding act.

Safety Depositories. These are strong, fire-proof vaults, constructed in connection with a business edifice, for the purpose of affording people the opportunity of depositing their money and other valuables therein. Have been and are all the time the repositories of millions of dollars in gold, silver and other money which are thus withdrawn from circulation.

Savings Banks. First established at Berne, in Switzerland, in 1787.

Seigniorage. A certain amount of toll levied by the government upon bullion, ostensibly for the purpose of covering the expense of coinage. Thus the difference in price between the cost of bullion and what it will sell for, when converted into coin, is seigniorage. Nickel, as a commodity, may be worth 70 cents a pound. When converted into nickel coins this pound is worth $5. The difference of $4.30, between the bullion and coin value, is seigniorage. The profits to the United States, during 1892, from silver seigniorage, were $930,630.90.

Sight Draft. This is used when the person upon whom it is drawn is expected to pay the debt immediately. In the time draft the same is made payable in a certain number of days.

Silver. Exists in most parts of the world, and through the introduction of improved machinery for crushing ore, in which it is found, and separating it from the same, has been produced in great abundance of late years. For 200 years it cost about as much to produce fifteen pounds of silver as to produce one of gold. More recently it is claimed that twenty-five pounds of silver can be obtained as easily as one pound of gold. Others deny that there would be an excess of silver were free coinage to prevail. See Free Coinage.

Silver Certificates. Consist of paper money in denominations of 1, 2, 5, 10, 20, 50, 100, 500 and 1,000 dollars and are given out at the United States treasury upon deposits of silver. These certificates are receivable for customs, taxes and all public dues.

Silver in Canada. Silver dollars in Canada are worth what can be obtained for them in the United States. Whatever passes at par in the United States should be nearly at par in Canada.

Silver in Great Britain. Table showing the average price of silver in London since 1873, the year when the mint bureau was created, and the equivalent in United States gold coin of an ounce fine at average price, gain or loss per cent, bullion values of a United States silver dollar, gain or loss per cent of the silver in a United States silver dollar, and the ratio of gold to silver:

Calendar year.	Value of fine ounce at average quotation.	Gain or loss per cent.	Bullion value of a U. S. silver dollar.	Gold ratio.
1873	$1.30	45 .. gain	$1.004	15.9
1874	1.28	1 .... loss	989	16.2
1875	1.25	3 .... loss	96	16.6
1876	1.16	10 .... loss	89	17.9
1877	1.20	.7 .... loss	92	17.2
1878	1.15	10 .loss	89	17.9
1879	1.12	13 .... loss	869	18.4
1880	1.14	11 .... loss	886	18.
1881	1.14	12 .... loss	88	18.1
1882	1.13	12 .... loss	878	18.2
1883	1.11	14 .... loss.	868	18.6
1884	1.11	14 .... loss	86	18.6
1885	1.06	18 .... loss	82	19 4
1886	99	23 .... loss	769	20.8
1887	98	24 .... loss	757	21.1
1888	94	27 .... loss	727	22.
1889	93	28 .... loss	72	22.
1890	1.05	19 .... loss	809	19.7
1891	99	23 .... loss	76	20.9
1892	87	33 .... loss	67	23.7
1893	8 mos.... 81	37 .... loss	625	25-5

Silver Question, of 1893, Explained. There are 12 ounces or 5,630 grains in a pound of silver, troy weight. There are $371\frac{1}{4}$ grains of pure silver in a dollar, and about 15 pure silver dollars are contained in a pound. The government, in 1893, bought silver bullion at 74 cents per ounce, which makes the cost of pure silver, contained in a pound, to be $8.88. One tenth of a dollar is an alloy of copper, which, at 10 cents a pound, makes the cost of copper in a dollar less than one cent. The expense of coining a dollar will not exceed one cent. Thus the cost to the government of purchasing the metal and making a pound of dollars is not over $8.90. When coined the pound of silver becomes worth $15. The profit to the government, which is termed seigniorage, on each pound of dollars, is $6.10. Differences of opinion exist as to whether silver should be remonetized, with free coinage at the ratio of 16 to 1. The silver advocates claim that with bimetallism and free coinage the financial conditions of the country were highly prosperous up to 1873. That since that time, when silver was demonetized, prices and values have steadily declined. To satisfy the claimants for silver the Bland Act was passed in 1878, which authorized the coinage of not less than two nor more than four millions of dollars per month. This Act was repealed in 1890 and the Sherman law enacted, which provided for the purchase of 4,500,000 ounces of silver monthly. With silver worth 74 cents per ounce, that made an expenditure, by the government, of $3,330,000 per month.

Although this amount of silver was paid for in silver certificates, the understanding prevailed that these certificates could be and were exchanged for gold; and in the early part of 1893, with the rapid outflow of gold to Europe, the impression prevailed that the country was losing all of its gold because of this continually large amount of silver being purchased. A financial panic followed which the advocates of a gold standard claimed could only be overcome by repealing the Sherman Act and stopping the further purchase of silver. The advocates of gold further claim that not more than about two dollars of silver coin per person can be circulated, in the United States, and that the piling up of 300 or 400 millions of dollars, in silver bullion, in the treasury vaults, for the sake of accommodating the silver mining interest is a piece of folly. The advocates of silver reply that this attempt to suppress the mining and purchase of silver is wholly in the interest of the banks and others who are large owners of gold. The gold advocates retort by saying, that with the great supplies of silver ore in sight and the improved facilities for mining silver it is liable to become as cheap as copper; and that we might just as well impose a law that the government should buy a certain amount of copper per month, and give out copper certificates, as to continue that arbitrary law in relation to silver. To this the silverite replies by asking why free coinage of gold? And why not free coinage of silver? To this the gold advocate replies by saying that gold, because of continued scarcity and general value, is the recognized standard throughout the civilized world. The friend of silver rejoins by saying that several of the most prosperous countries on the earth use only silver as a metal standard, while others use gold and silver; and further that no evidence exists that the common people, in any country, having an exclusive gold standard, are more prosperous than those elsewhere. Sherman law repealed Nov. 1, 1893.

Sinking Fund. A fund created for sinking, or paying a public debt.

Specie Payments. Were suspended in the United States from 1861 to 1879. Gold went up to $2.85 in 1864. Specie payments were resumed January 1, 1879.

Sterling. Relating to coinage in the British Empire. The word is supposed to have been derived from Esterling, the name of a family of early money dealers in England.

. Stocks. Property invested in shares of such character as can be bought and sold. Railroad shares, bank shares, shares in numerous corporations, and many public properties, when placed in the market, are known as stocks, which fluctuate in price, according to the dividends they pay. Bonds differ from stocks, in that they pay a regular interest until such time as the bond matures, when the principal sum, named in the bond, is supposed to be paid. The stockholder has a vote in the control of his stock. The bondholder has no vote on the stock, but he draws interest regularly, his bond being in the nature of a mortgage.

Subsidiary Silver Coins. Are the small coins made of silver in denominations less than one dollar. Such coins have been issued, in the United States, to the amount of $78,000,000 and constitute about 5 per cent of the total money of the country. Subsidiary silver comprises about 14 per cent of the total money of Great Britain, 5 per cent of Italy, and 11 per cent of Germany. Supposing it to average 10 per cent of the world's money there would be about $1,000,000,000 of subsidiary silver coin on earth, being one-quarter of the total silver coinage on the globe.

Trade Dollar. Silver dollars coined of such weight as will be acceptable and will readily pass in trade in foreign countries. Such dollars usually contained more silver than the United States standard silver dollar; but instead of passing current in this country, were worth only their bullion value, which was less than the value of the standard dollar.

Treasury Notes. Paper money authorized to be paid by the treasurer of the United States in the purchase of silver bullion, such notes to be redeemed by the treasurer on demand in gold or silver at his discretion. They resemble the national bank note in general appearance and are in denominations of 1, 2, 5, 10, 20, 50, 100, 500 and 1,000 dollars.

Troy Weight. The present ounce was brought from Grand Cairo into Europe, in 1095, and was adopted at Troyes, a city of France, whence the name. Is used to weigh only gold, silver and precious stones. The following is the table:

32 grains 1 carat, diamond weight.
24 grains 1 pennyweight.
20 pennyweights 1 ounce.
12 ounces 1 pound.

United States Notes. Paper money notes which are made receivable in payment of all taxes, internal duties, excises, debts, and demands of any kind, due to the United States, and of all claims and demands against the United States, of any kind whatsoever. They are also known as legal tender notes, being in denominations 1, 2, 5, 10, 20, 50, 100, 500, and 1,000 dollars.

Warehouse Receipts. These are certificates of deposit indicating that certain grains or commodities like pig iron, tin, zinc, stoves or other goods, having marketable value, are stored in the warehouse. On such receipts the banks will lend money to the extent of thirty, forty or fifty per cent of their value, more or less.

REFORMERS, ATTENTION!

REFORM LECTURERS interested in the live issue of Government ownership of banks, who endorse the plan proposed in this volume, are earnestly invited to call upon or correspond with the publishers of this book.

ALL REFORMERS, heads of labor organizations and others, who believe in Government ownership of banks, who wish to organize clubs, and would like to arrange for visits from organizers and lecturers, will please address the publishers. All persons who are in sympathy with the purpose of this book and wish to sell or distribute copies, are invited to write for terms by the dozen, hundred or thousand. If you cannot do this work yourself, can you not help some one else by bringing it to his attention?

SALESMEN AND SALESWOMEN wanted in every neighborhood to take orders for this book. The education of the people and the adoption of the suggestions here made will bring settled monetary conditions and prosperity for all. The people are ready and waiting for these ideas. The book will sell itself. Address for terms,

CHARLES H. KERR & COMPANY, Publishers,
175 Monroe Street, CHICAGO.

Profit Sharing Realized.

An investment of $1.00 a month, for 10 months, will purchase a business opportunity that will give good direct returns and remunerative employment for spare moments.

THE BOOK PUBLISHING BUSINESS of Charles H. Kerr & Company was established in 1886, and has gradually been built up until it carries on its list of publications nearly a hundred different books, with an annual output of from fifteen to twenty new books each year. The list covers a wide variety of subjects, including science, poetry, fiction, philosophy, religion, essays, etc., but the main endeavor of the house is increasingly in the direction of books that help the struggle of the oppressed for fairer social conditions. "The Coming Climax," by Lester C. Hubbard, sounded a note of alarm and appealed to the prosperous middle classes to join the workers against the monopolists who are the enemies of both. "An Ounce of Prevention," by Augustus Jacobson, points out the expediency of a succession tax to do away with the great fortunes that are an ever-increasing menace to society. Mr. Van Ornum's books show clearly how the individualistic remedy for corrupt legislation may be applied when once the people are aroused. Helen Gardener's "Facts and Fictions of Life" exposes the inhumanity of the law as it affects the unfortunate and points out what woman can do to help the life of the future. Mr. Hill's "Money Found" shows how the nationalization of the banks would remove one of the worst causes of poverty and immensely increase the well being of the people. "Washington Brown, Farmer," by LeRoy Armstrong, gives a great lesson in co-operation to the farmers in the course of a story of thrilling interest. Two new novels are now ready: "A Modern Love

Story," which leaves its theme long enough to strike some sturdy blows at capitalistic oppression, and "From Earth's Center," which describes a Utopia where the single tax has worked out its healthful results, the destruction of monopoly, the preservation of individual liberty. But we must refer readers to our catalogue, or better, to the books themselves, for a full idea of the scope of our publications.

PRINTING PLANT. In 1893 a favorable opportunity was offered for adding a plant of typesetting machines, and this is now a valuable portion of the assets of the business. The plant has the capacity for turning out each week over 500 plates for the printing of book pages, has already nearly paid for itself out of the profits of composition, and promises to be a steady source of revenue in addition to the profits on sales of books

CAPITALIZATION. In 1893, for the sake of introducing the profit sharing principle, the business was incorporated with 1,000 shares of $10 each, nearly 900 of which are still controlled by the original owner. The property represented by these shares includes the copyrights, plates and editions of the books in the catalogue, besides the printing plant already described.

PRIVILEGES OF STOCKHOLDERS. All who are familiar with the process of making books will understand that apart from the royalty paid to the author, there are two important elements in the cost of each book. Taking for example a book of 300 pages which retails for one dollar, the cost of typesetting and electrotyping, which must be paid before the first book is ready, would be about $300, while the cost of making each copy after the first might not exceed 22 cents. Thus if the sales can be largely increased, there is a fair profit at much less than the regular prices. We have therefore decided to offer to our stockholders and those subscribing for stock, any cloth books published by us, *prepaid*, at three-fifths the advertised prices, and any paper books published by us, *prepaid*, at one-half the advertised prices.

CLASS OF STOCKHOLDERS DESIRED. Only 400 shares of stock are in the market. We desire to place these with persons who are directly interested in the circulation of books of social reform. Such persons will find the shares trebly profitable, first, in reducing the cost of the social reform and miscellaneous books required for their own reading; second, in the large margin of profit on such books as they may have leisure to sell, at the same time promoting the cause they have at heart; third, in the regular dividends on stock, which we confidently predict will not be less than 8 per cent after this year.

TERMS OF PURCHASE. The price of shares is $10 00 each. To bring them within the reach of all, we offer them for $1.00 cash and $1.00 payable on or before the 10th day of each month until the whole is paid. Each remittance will be acknowledged, and a paid up certificate of stock will be furnished when the whole amount has been paid. To those who prefer to save clerical work by paying the $10.00 cash in advance, we will give as a premium a year's subscription to NEW OCCASIONS or a dollar's worth of books at catalogue prices.

NO LIABILITY. Our company is organized under the Illinois law, so that when a share of stock is paid for, the stockholder can never be held liable in any way on account of the corporation.

RESPONSIBILITY. We invite the fullest investigation into our responsibility, and refer inquirers to any houses with whom we do business. Our electrotypers are Blomgren Bros. & Co., 175 Monroe Street, our binders the Thomas Knapp Printing and Binding Co., 347 Dearborn Street, our paper is bought mostly from George H. Taylor & Co. and the Chicago Paper Company, and our banking is done with the Merchant's Loan and Trust Company, F. N. Wilder, ass't cashier. We also take pleasure in referring to Hon. Thos. E. Hill, Glen Ellyn, Ill.. the author of Hill's Manual, whose recent book "Money Found," published by us, is meeting with rapid sale wherever it is introduced.

Remittances should be made by express money orders where possible, otherwise by postal order or bank draft. Postal notes are at senders' risk. Address

Charles H. Kerr & Co., Publishers,

175 Monroe Street, Chicago.

BLANK APPLICATION FOR STOCK.

Charles H. Kerr & Company,
175 Monroe Street, Chicago,

Gentlemen: I hereby subscribe for one share of stock in your company at $10.00, which find enclosed. I wish as a premium for advance payment

....

[Cross out the preceding paragraph or the following, according to to amount of money enclosed.]

I hereby subscribe for one share of stock in your company at $10.00. I enclose $1.00 herewith, and agree to pay one dollar on or before the tenth day of each calendar month after this date until the whole is paid.

It is understood that in consideration of the amount paid I am to have the option of purchasing all books published by you at the rate of one half retail prices for paper books and three fifths retail prices for cloth books, including prepayment of charges by you.

Address

ASLEEP AND AWAKE,
A Realistic Story of Chicago.

Raymond Russell is the name on the title page. Raymond Russell is the hero of the story, or rather the lover of the heroine. The real author is a Chicago writer who has published other well known books, but whose identity the publishers are not yet at liberty to disclose.

Leonore, the heroine, is a girl living in a country town, whose intellectual nature is awakened by a chance meeting with Raymond Russell. She comes to Chicago without his knowledge, and having a remarkable voice, aims at a musical career. But she finds every door closed to her. Her money is gone, and after a vain wandering in search of work, she faints on the crowded street. The one person who takes pity on her is Adel, a "fallen" woman of Custom House Place. Here the scene of the remainder of the book is laid, and the reader follows the story with breathless interest up to the tragic climax.

The author comments unsparingly on the double standard of morals applied to the male and the female frequenters of the scenes described, yet refutes the indiscriminate charges of Count Tolstoi against men.

Every one who read the Kreutzer Sonata should read "Asleep and Awake," where after the worst has been said, new ground is given for faith in a pure love, not in woman alone but in man.

12mo, handsome cloth binding, one dollar postpaid.

CHARLES H. KERR & COMPANY, Publishers,
175 Monroe Street, Chicago.

Commendations of "Money Found."

The following are gathered at random from a great mass of commendatory mention of the first edition of this book. This second edition, containing the glossary of financial terms, it is seen, is a great improvement over the first issue.

Will appeal to those who have large faith in "government."—Hamlin Garland in THE ARENA.

I think "Money Found" is the best reform book published.—J. X. DUVAL, 103 Second street, Manchester, N. H.

Ought to be read by every person who would understand the question of finance.—ALMA NEWS, Alma, Kan.

Let every speaker, every instructor on financial reform procure a copy of this book.—EXPRESS, Chicago.

We wish every voter in the country would read this book. It will give you new ideas.—RENVILLE CO. UNION, Minn.

The propositions in this book are bound to set the reader to thinking. It has pretty nearly converted us to the idea that government banks are feasible and practicable.—THE WORKMAN, Grand Rapids, Mich.

The book is thoughtful and well written by a man of large information. Will open the eyes of people to the evil of the present banking system and will prepare the way for something better. It should have a sale of a million copies in the next three months.—PEOPLE'S VOICE, Imperial, Neb.

If our Congress would drop that old granny whim of "intrinsic value" and institute a new system of banking, proposed by Thos. E. Hill, the country would rise out of this panic and leap to the front in less time than it takes congress to argue this silver question.—LEADER, Groton, S. Dak.

An exposition of the principles of government finance I have believed in for years. How much for 100 copies can you furnish the book should I take it in my head to do some missionary work in that line? I think it more important than our *religious* work, eh?—REV. H. LEWELLEN, West Union, Iowa.

A masterly treatise on the financial question.—HERALD, Good Thunder, Minn.

This plan for banking is sensible and plainly stated.—A. W. Landon, in Chicago HUMANE JOURNAL.

Though simple it is elaborate and leaves no point unexplained.—JEWELL Co. NEWS, Jewell, Kan.

Does not attempt a revolution in existing conditions, but adapts itself to the limitations of the present day.—EVENING LAMP, Chicago.

Especially does the work commend itself to those of the prudent middle and laboring classes, whose savings are at present jeopardized by the uncertainty of our banking laws.—CHRISTIAN CYNOSURE, Chicago.

The cleverest and most forcible presentation of the money question we have seen. It is an overwhelming and unanswerable argument in favor of government ownership of the banking system and ought to be read by every citizen.—THE LEADER, Wichita, Kan.

The entire work is replete with new and sensible ideas. May we live to see its principles in active operation in the near future. We advise every voter to procure a copy, to thoroughly peruse its pages and then vote for the principles it advocates.—AMERICAN ENTERPRISE, East Hartford, Conn.

It settles the question of gold and silver parity, as well as other issues, which have recently vexed the brains of honest industry; this plan not being to tinker up our banking system, already too complex and carrying too much dead weight, but to substitute in its place a currency that no one can object to, except the few who are reaping a harvest, as speculative custodians of the people's money.—RUFUS BLANCHARD, Chicago.

All letters from persons who approve the plan proposed in this book, for government ownership of banks, will be welcomed at the office of publication.

If desirous of entering actively upon the work of reforming our monetary system, please see the request, made on page 122, headed "Reformers Attention!"

www.ingramcontent.com/pod-product-compliance
Lightning Source LLC
Chambersburg PA
CBHW030615270326
41927CB00007B/1187